DEATH BEFORE DYING

Death Before Dying

The Sufi Poems of
SULTAN BAHU

Translated and introduced by
JAMAL J. ELIAS

UNIVERSITY OF CALIFORNIA PRESS
Berkeley   Los Angeles   London

University of California Press
Berkeley and Los Angeles, California

University of California Press, Ltd.
London, England

© 1998 by
The Regents of the University of California

Library of Congress Cataloging-in-Publication Data

Sulṭān Bāhū, 1630–1691.
    [Poems. English Selections]
    Death before dying : the Sufi poems of Sultan Bahu / translated
and introduced by Jamal J. Elias.
        p.   cm.
    Includes bibliographical references (p.   ) and index.
    ISBN 0-520-21135-9 (cloth : alk. paper).—ISBN 0-520-21242-8
(pbk. : alk. paper)
    1. Sufi poetry, Punjabi—Translations into English. I. Elias, Jamal J.
II. Title.
PK2656.5.E5A6 1998
891.4'213—dc21   97-19194

The paper used in this publication meets the minimum requirements of
American National Standard for Information Sciences—Permanence of Paper
for Printed Library Materials, ANSI Z39.48-1984.

for Danielle,

those who do not lose their treasures do not find a friend

CONTENTS

ACKNOWLEDGMENTS

I would like to express my deepest gratitude to Danielle C. Elias and Shahzad Bashir for not only encouraging this project but also for carefully and critically reading my translations; to my father for introducing me to Sultan Bahu; to my mother for making Punjabi sound lyrical; and to Begum Abida Parveen and Ustad Pathana Khan, neither of whom I have had the pleasure of meeting, for making Bahu's *Abyāt* come alive through song.

INTRODUCTION

POETRY ENJOYS PRIDE OF PLACE among literary and artistic forms throughout the Islamic world. While this is no doubt due in part to its aesthetics, the mnemonic quality of poetry makes it easy to remember for people who cannot read and write—a significant proportion of the world's Muslim population today as in the past. It is simultaneously valued for the same characteristics by literate people, for, as something that you can carry in your memory, it is a cheap and portable form of art.

One of the most satisfying marriages in world literature is the one between Islamic mystical (Sufi) experiences and teachings and poetry, which is capable of conveying these ideas in a manner that is as seductive as it is instructive. The mystical poetry written in Persian by famous figures such as Rumi (d. 1273), Saʿdi (d. 1292), and Hafiz (d. 1389) is very well known both in the Persian original and in its celebrated and widely circulated translations. But mystical poetry is composed and enjoyed to no less a degree in other languages spoken by Muslims all over the world. There is a rich tradition of Sufi literary composition in Arabic which is often used as a source of inspiration by the best known Persian poets. Similarly, Ottoman Turkish and Urdu poetry derive much of their literary style from Persian and much of their content from both Arabic and Persian alongside their native Turkish and Indian cultures.

Persian Sufi poetry and its derivative genres in Urdu and Ottoman Turkish are representatives of a highly literate court culture, and have traditionally enjoyed a limited audience outside these circles. Paralleling this "high culture" form of poetry there was a popular Sufi poetical literature in both Punjabi and other languages spoken by Indian Muslims (not to mention Arabic, vernacular Turkish, Kurdish, and many others). This form of poetry was often viewed as too rustic to enjoy court patronage, and received none of the encouragement or rewards enjoyed by "high culture" poetry. It is therefore a testament to the innate talents of these popular Sufi poets and to the magnetic attraction of their poetry that for every Ottoman court poet like Sheyh Galip there is a Yunus Emre, and for every Mughal court figure like Mirza Ghalib there is a Sultan Bahu.

In fact, it is these popular poets, writing in the vernaculars of their own people, who are more renowned. The average citizen of a small town in Anatolia may not even be familiar with Sheyh Galip's name, but more than likely would know some of Yunus Emre's poetry by heart. Similarly, an ordinary citizen of the Punjab is unlikely to be familiar with Mirza Ghalib's work, but could be moved to tears by listening to someone like Sultan Bahu.

BAHU'S RELIGIOUS MESSAGE

Sultan Bahu's mystical poetry is an expression of disillusionment with formal, legalistic, and institutionalized forms of religion, and of optimistic faith in the possibility of a personal, individual spiritual relationship with God. Bahu is emphasizing a central tenet of Sufism: that an absolute love for and devotion to God can result in the experience of losing oneself within the divine. The major impediment to this union is human attachment to the physical world, an instinct ingrained in the human soul. Through systematic detachment from this world and the practice of asceticism under the guidance of a Sufi master—together with meditational exercises based on the repetition of God's name—the Sufi successfully tames the soul. The soul's passions, once harnessed, help transport the Sufi further along his or her journey. The imagery used is often that of taming a horse, which then becomes the mount on which the mystic travels for the rest of the mystical path. The ultimate goal of this journey is to lose one's identity within the greater identity of God, or to attain spiritual death before physical death. This quest for death before dying is based on a saying attributed to the Prophet: "Die before you die!"

Sultan Bahu develops these central concepts in a manner which would be appealing and accessible to a wide audience unfamiliar with the more esoteric and philosophical dimensions of Sufism. He emphasizes the power of love and stresses that love is more important than learning. In order to show the danger of turning religious practice into a habit or a birthright, he juxtaposes the learned scholar, who is incapable of attaining God, against the illiterate person whose love-madness transports him or her to the divine.

> The Lord was neither found on the exalted throne, nor is the Lord in the Ka'ba.
> The Lord was not found in learning and books, nor is the Lord in the prayer niche.
> He was never found swimming in the Ganges, nor met through countless pilgrimages.[1]

In line with many other Sufi figures from the formative period of Sufism in the ninth century onward, Bahu uses an emphasis on the value of illiteracy not to undermine the importance of Islam as a religion but to underline it. According to Bahu, while religious scholars only observe the formal, outward aspects of Islamic ritual and doctrine, the illiterate lover understands their true meaning. In

3

the heart of the lover, the Islamic creedal statement "There is no god but Allah, and Muhammad is the messenger of Allah" takes on a magical significance. Bahu states that the only writing one needs to know are the letters *mīm* and *alif*. The *mīm* is the first letter of the name "Muhammad." The *alif* is the first letter of the Arabic alphabet and also the first letter of the name "Allah." It is written as a vertical line, bringing to mind a raised index finger and symbolizing the unity of God. Thus when Bahu speaks of knowing only the *alif*, he is positioning himself squarely in a Sufi tradition which uses this metaphor to emphasize the futility of becoming preoccupied with external forms while ignoring underlying meanings.

> Those who find the Beloved in the letter *alif* need not open the
> Qur'an to read it.[2]

Many of Sultan Bahu's metaphors are common to Sufi poetry in many languages. The divine beloved is haughty and distant, and the quest for this beloved is a source of great anguish to the Sufi lover. The lover is likened to a nightingale in love with the rose which sits unattainable in its bed of thorns, causing the nightingale to spend its life in lamentation and to risk capture in the rose garden of grief:

> I pecked and ate many grains of wheat, now the string of eternity is
> around my neck.
> I flutter, caught in the noose, like the nightingale in the garden.[3]

Such metaphors and his references to famous Sufi figures of the past also place him squarely in a wider Sufi poetical tradition, as does his use of the term *faqir* (meaning beggar) to refer to a mystic, thus signifying the belief that material poverty is related to spiritual wealth.

Sufi symbolism is apparent in Bahu's very name, which means "with Him" (i.e., God). Bahu used his given name to greater advantage than most other poets. Most of his poems end in the refrain "hu" ("He" or "Him"), a formula which simultaneously renders them instantly recognizable as Sultan Bahu's compositions and marks them as specifically Sufi poetry because "hu" is a common formula in the Sufi meditational exercise of *zikr*. This refrain became so characteristic of his style that later generations added it to all his poems. In a similar fashion, his name "Bahu" appears in the final line of all his poems, even though in many instances it ruins the meter of the verse and was, undoubtedly, not included by the poet himself. On other occasions, not only is the name Bahu an integral part of the final verse, as is common in Islamic poetic traditions, but its meaning is also incorporated into the poem:

> You will find the singular Beloved if you gamble your head.
> Be drunk in the love of Allah, always saying "Hu! Hu!"
> While contemplating the name of Allah, control your breath.
> When essence blends with Essence, only then will you be called "Bahu."[4]

Many of the themes discussed by Bahu and the metaphors he uses are drawn from the literary bank of Sufi writing and are then adapted to the Punjabi environment. A striking example of this is his frequent reference to birds. In addition to the stock metaphor of the nightingale referred to above, Bahu made particular use of hawks and falcons. They are often used as symbols of the soul in its quest to return to God, just as a falcon desires to return to its master's hand:

> How can the poor falcon fly, for its feet have been bound.
> Whoever does not possess love, Bahu, loses both worlds.[5]

In some of his poems Bahu refers to birds in a context which is comprehensible only if one is familiar with the Indian environment. This is true, for example, in his reference to the owl as symbolizing stupidity[6] and in his images of birds singing as if to welcome the monsoon:

> I wander lamenting like the cuckoo, begging that my days not go by
> in waste.
> Speak, bird! The monsoon has come; perhaps God will shed some
> rain.[7]

The cuckoo is traditionally believed to be singing a lament that means "Where is my beloved?" In the second line, I have substituted the generic "bird" for a species known as *papeeha* in Punjabi, the call of which is this same lament.

— Bahu's extreme reverence for his spiritual master is also a theme common in Sufism, particularly in the Indian context. Sufi writers traditionally emphasize the centrality of a living spiritual guide, stating that it is almost impossible to attain advanced mystical states without the help of such a master. The Sufi practitioner is supposed to surrender both his body and soul to this person, proverbially becoming like a corpse in the hands of a mortician. This attitude toward Sufi masters has led to a very high degree of veneration, so much so that the tombs of dead Sufis function as the centers of saint and shrine cults which are visited by all sorts of devotees, most of whom have no formal Sufi affiliation. They also function as the centers for major religious celebrations, and many people come to these shrines to seek the intercession of Sufi saints—both living and dead—for critical events in their lives. Many legalistic scholars find this veneration suspect and speak out against the Sufi shrines. In premodern times such critics had limited success in curtailing the popular devotion to Sufi shrines, which occupy a more central position in the spiritual landscape of the Punjab and other parts of South Asia than do the mosques. Bahu echoes this sentiment in his many verses which assert that devotion to a Sufi guide is a substitute for the literal observance of all Islamic rituals:

> This body is a dwelling of the true Lord, and my heart like a garden
> in bloom.
> Within it are fountains, within it are prayer grounds, within it places
> to bow down in prayer.
> Within it is the Ka'ba, within it the *qibla,* within it cries of "Only
> Allah!"
> I found the Perfect Guide, Bahu, He alone will take care of me.[8]

One of the most intriguing features of Bahu's poetry, also characteristic of popular Sufi poetry in India, is his occasional use of the feminine gender when talking about himself. Sufi love poetry outside India (and even in the Indian high culture traditions of Persian and Urdu) represents the relationship between lover and beloved as one in which an active human lover pursues a passive (or passive-aggressive) beloved. This dynamic traditionally genders the active partner as male. There is some ambiguity concerning the gender of the passive partner, in part because homoerotic love is widely accepted in Islamic literature and in part because of the lack of formal gender in both Persian and Ottoman. Most of Sultan Bahu's poems fit this pattern, but in a few of them the lover is explicitly female, something which is very clear since Punjabi does have gender:

> I am ugly and my Beloved beautiful—how can I be agreeable
> to Him?
> He never enters my home though I use a hundred thousand ruses.
> Neither am I beautiful nor have I wealth to display—how can I
> please my Friend?
> This pain shall remain forever, Bahu, I will die crying.[9]

There is little Islamic precedent for this form of eroticization of the relationship between the human being and God. On the other hand, it seems to share many elements with Hindu literature, in particular with the *virāhinī* tradition of northern India in which the poet addresses God in the voice of a girl or young woman.[10] Similar to the devotional love poets of the *bhakti* tradition of Krishnaite Hinduism, the Sufi poet can be seen in the role of the herdswoman or Gopi who is in love with God. The death anniversary of an Indian Sufi saint is traditionally called an *'urs,* an Arabic word for "wedding," and many of the rituals undertaken at such festivals clearly celebrate the saint's death as the occasion of his marriage to God. Such feminization of the Sufi is taken to an extreme in some popular Sufi groups where the men dress up in women's clothing. Bahu evokes this image in one of his poems where he uses the term *sadā suhāgan* to indicate a level of blessed happiness; the term literally means a woman whose husband never dies and who therefore never becomes a widow.[11]

Some of the images evoked by Sultan Bahu are peculiar to his Indian environment. Islam and Hinduism were viewed by many legalistic religious scholars as mutually irreconcilable religious systems. This attitude sometimes combined with the administrative policies of Muslim rulers to create conditions of mutual hostility between Muslims and Hindus. It was largely through the efforts of mystical figures such as Sultan Bahu that Islam gained popularity and converts in India. These mystical thinkers not only absorbed Indian ideas and values, they also consciously attempted to address an audience wider than the Turco–Persian settlers and the small number of Persianized Indian converts. Sultan Bahu's Punjabi poetry is clear evidence of this. The majority of his works are in Persian, but his fame derives from Punjabi verses that emphasize the sincerity of religious devotion irrespective of religious affiliation. It is no wonder that he is revered by Sikh and Hindu Punjabis as well as by Muslims.

The Punjabi language has languished in comparison to the change in status of other northern Indian languages in the last two hundred years. Before the British colonization of India, its Muslim rulers had used Persian as their official language and ignored local vernaculars. Following the breakup of the Mughal Empire, the Sikh rulers of the Punjab continued to favor Persian as the language of state despite the fact that Punjabi is the Sikh scriptural language. By the time the British finally conquered the Punjab in 1839–41, the British administrative policy of using major ethnic languages to communicate with the colonized population was well in place, and the choice of Urdu (a language from north-central India) as the administrative language of Indian Muslims was an accomplished fact.

It is therefore no surprise that when British colonial rule was extended to the Punjab, Urdu was used as the medium of official commerce with the Punjabi Muslims (the use of Persian, the Islamic imperial language, was simply never an option for the British). As a movement for Muslim self-determination took shape in northern India, the majority of Muslim activists, including those from the Punjab, willingly accepted Urdu as the language representing Muslim ethnicity. This pattern, in which Punjabi was marginalized and trivialized to the benefit of Urdu, continued after the establishment of Pakistan in 1947.[12] The trivialization of Punjabi has meant that the government, which is the main sponsor of educational and cultural projects, has put virtually no effort into the standardization of Punjabi as a language or the preservation and dissemination of its literature. There is no standardized Punjabi grammar or script, and no good Punjabi dictionary. As a result systematic, critical studies of Punjabi literary works are all but impossible to do.

Greater Punjab is a vast geographical region, including the dusty flat lands surrounding Delhi, the rolling hills of Jammu and Himachal Pradesh, the narrow valleys of Hazara and Azad Kashmir, the salt hills and scrub of the Potohar plateau, and the rocky desert of the Deras in Baluchistan, Sindh, and Sarhad (the anachronistic North West Frontier Province of Pakistan). But the Punjabi heartland is the northwestern corner of the Indo-Gangetic plain, a flat region dominated by its rivers and from which the Punjab (Five Rivers) takes its name. Most of Islamic Punjabi literature comes from the center of this region, a place known as the Rechna Doab (Ravi and Chenab Twin River Region).

The rivers dictate the rhythms of the romanticized Punjabi life. The major daily occupations of this life are farming and the care of cows and water buffaloes. People live in villages surrounded by fields, rather than in homesteads located on private land. As a result, the daily march out to the fields or to pastures has become a motif in Punjabi literature. The rivers and the agriculture dependent upon them become the context in which the dramatic moments of Punjabi life are played out. Bathing, washing clothes and fetching water, grazing animals, fetching fodder, meeting mystics and mendicants, taking food to farmers and herdsmen—all become scenes of romance and intrigue. The Punjab is a place where poets can evoke images of birds pecking out the newly sprouted shoots of wheat, where buffaloes refuse to yield their milk until they hear the flute of their herdsman, and where (as mentioned earlier) a variety of lark is named after its plaintive cry, "Where is my beloved?"

This is a place where the rivers flood their banks with every monsoon, and where they mysteriously change course as they make their serpentine way from the Himalayas to the Arabian Sea. As the rivers make new channels, they create rich alluvial islands, called "belas." The bela is an important part of life as recorded in Punjabi literature. A good *bela* is covered with grass, a bad *bela* with marshes and quicksand; a good *bela* is a place to graze animals and meet lovers, a bad *bela* is where tigers hunt and where one dies of snakebite or drowning. It is on a *bela* that Hir meets her beloved Ranjha in the famous Punjabi epic, and it is on the *bela* that she is betrayed. Thus when Sultan Bahu uses the imagery of the *bela,* he is not only evoking all that the *bela* represents in Punjabi rural life, he is also drawing on his audience's familiarity with the image of the *bela* in Punjabi literature, particularly in the epic of Hir.[13]

It is in the wedding of Islamic mystical metaphors with the imagery of the Punjabi heartland that Sultan Bahu most distinguishes himself, and it is in this very aspect that I feel my translations are weakest. Assuming that the majority of readers of this work will be unfamiliar not only with Punjabi but also with the Punjab, I have leaned toward more generic metaphors in my translation. Thus "*bela*" is translated as "marsh," "dune," and "river bank." I have also changed the names of birds and plants when the original is unknown in most of the English-speaking world. In other places, I have taken advantage of linguistic ambiguity, such as in translating the word *daryā* as either "sea" or "river" depending on the context.

I have attempted to translate Bahu's work as literally as possible while retaining some semblance of English style and grammar. One characteristic of the genre of Punjabi *abyāt* is that the content of each line of a poem does not necessarily have anything to do with the next. Furthermore, Bahu's *Abyāt* are often in a very colloquial tone, and frequently reverse the normal Punjabi word order. These characteristics combine to give the translation an occasionally choppy and awkward tone. Keeping in mind the fact that these poems are normally sung, and are not expected to conform strictly to Indo-Persian metrics, I have rearranged the sentence structure only in a few extreme cases. The Punjabi *Abyāt* of Sultan Bahu are normally arranged in alphabetical order by the first letter of the Arabo-Persian alphabet. Since this arrangement is irrelevant in an English translation and has absolutely no relationship to the content, I have arranged the translations according to my own aesthetic sense.

SULTAN BAHU'S LIFE

Very little is known about Sultan Bahu's life, and such information as exists is shaped by a three-hundred-year-long exercise in hagiography. He is mentioned in passing in biographical dictionaries of Indian Sufi figures, but these entries are extremely brief. The only substantial account of his life is in the *Manāqib-i Sultānī,* a work written six or seven generations after Sultan Bahu's death by one of his descendants by the name of Sultan Hamid. According to this text, which is extremely hagiographical in its tone, Sultan Bahu was born during the reign of the Mughal ruler Shah Jahan (r. 1628–58) in the town of Shorkot, located between Multan and Jhang in Pakistan. Shorkot had been given as a source of revenue to his father, Bayazid Muhammad, in recognition for military service to the Mughal government. His mother, Rasti, gave him the overtly mystical name of Bahu, meaning "With Him [God]." Bahu kept this as his pen name, to which his disciples added the honorific title of "Sultan" which has been retained by both his spiritual and biological descendants. Prose works by Sultan Bahu suggest that he referred to himself as Bahu A'wan. The A'wans are a tribe, based in the extreme western end of the Punjab, claiming descent from 'Ali (the cousin and son-in-law of the Prophet) through his son Muhammad ibn al-Hanafiyya. 'Ali is considered the fourth caliph by Sunni and the first imam by Shi'a Muslims. As a result, not only do the A'wans command high status in the Indian Muslim environment for being Arabs but they also claim descent from the household of the Prophet, albeit not through his daughter Fatima.

Nothing is known of Sultan Bahu's early childhood or education. It has traditionally been held that he received little or no formal schooling, and evidence in support of this view is drawn from some of his verses. Such verses are a formulaic part of the image of the love-infused Sufi; they deemphasize formal education in order to underline the transformative power of the love of God. Stories abound of early Sufis who could read nothing except the name of God but who worked miracles through it. Bahu's extensive writings would, in fact, suggest that he must have had at least some formal schooling. His lengthy and esoteric Persian writings show that he was familiar with the standardized Sufi teachings of the day. Furthermore, Bahu's prose works contain many traditions of the Prophet which are quoted in Arabic, a language and literature which could only be learned in the Punjab through formal education.

The *Manāqib-i Sultānī* states that Sultan Bahu tried his hand at agriculture in his youth but gave it up and began to wander the forests and graveyards near Jhang. On one such occasion he encountered a Sufi on the banks of the Ravi. This man, named Habibullah Khan, became Bahu's first spiritual guide but quickly realized Bahu's unusual mystical potential and sent him to Delhi to study with his own master, Sayyid 'Abdur-Rahman of the Qadiri Sufi order. It is most likely that Bahu's formal knowledge of Sufism derives from the unspecified amount of time he spent in Delhi with this second Sufi master.

During his time in Delhi, Bahu met the future Mughal ruler Aurangzeb at least once at the communal Friday prayer. Some biographers have made much of his contact with Aurangzeb, the last of the truly powerful Mughals, but these contacts are no doubt exaggerated. Bahu does not appear to have wielded any influence over Aurangzeb's religious policies, nor did he benefit financially or politically from association with the future emperor. If anything, their relationship was most likely shaped by the fact that Bahu's Sufi master, Sayyid 'Abdur-Rahman, was related by marriage to Aurangzeb's estranged brother, Dara Shikuh. It is therefore unlikely that Sayyid 'Abdur-Rahman or any of his disciples would have had much to do with Aurangzeb.

Neither the date nor the reason for Bahu's return to Shorkot are known. The *Manāqib-i Sultānī* states that he married four times, had eight sons (daughters are not mentioned), and never again left the section of the Punjab from which he came. He died in 1691 and was buried outside Shorkot at a place called Qilaqahrgan (or Qilaqaʿr-gan). In 1775 the Chenab river changed course and threatened to wash away his grave, whereupon his coffin was dug up and moved to its present location where his shrine functions as a pilgrimage site for people from all over the Punjab.

SULTAN BAHU'S WRITTEN WORKS

Sultan Bahu's fame is almost entirely due to his Punjabi poetry, called the *Abyāt*. This is despite the fact that he was a prolific writer of Persian prose and poetry.[14] The author of the *Manāqib-i Sultānī* claims that Bahu wrote one hundred forty works, and twenty-six existing works are ascribed to him.[15] Most of these have been published as nonscholarly Urdu translations. Through a strange set of circumstances, the work of critical edition and study of the Persian texts is being thwarted by the heirs of one Malik Fazl Din who, in the first quarter of this century, came to the realization that his vocation in life was to disseminate the teachings of Sultan Bahu. Malik Fazl Din convinced the owners of what are believed to be the most accurate (and in some cases, the only known) manuscripts of Sultan Bahu's works to hand them over to him. He then commissioned a number of unskilled translators to render them into Urdu, which he published in a press he had opened in Lahore under the name

Allāh wālē kī qawmī dukkān (The Godly One's Public Shop). The original manuscripts are in the hands of Malik Fazl Din's family which allows no one, not even the spiritual heirs of Sultan Bahu, to see them.

This is very unfortunate, because the available translations suggest that Sultan Bahu's prose works are deserving of study. They are comprised of a number of book-length monographs and a majority of shorter treatises, containing general Sufi teachings, statements demonstrating the excellence of the Qadiri order, and didactic writings illustrating visions, stations, and states encountered along the Sufi path. A preliminary investigation suggests that the most important of these are *Mahik al-faqr kalān* and *Nūr al-huda-yi kalān*.

THE PUNJABI *ABYĀT*

Bahu excelled as a mystical poet. There are frequent and extensive fragments of Persian poetry in his prose works, and he also has a Persian collection of poetry which has been published together with a versified Urdu translation.[16] But his Persian verse has not gained a popularity in any way comparable to his Punjabi poetry, which is re-garded as one of the literary treasures of the language. At least four-teen editions of Bahu's Punjabi *Abyāt* have been printed, in both the Perso-Arabic and the Gurmukhi scripts (the latter being the script used by Sikhs). It has also been translated into Urdu and English, al-though all the translations have serious shortcomings.

Many problems of translation and redaction derive from the fact that there are no manuscripts of Bahu's Punjabi poetry known to predate this century. In fact, the oldest available collection of his *Abyāt* is a lithograph edition printed in 1891 and containing 116 po-ems. The most influential edition was published in 1915 by the aforementioned Malik Fazl Din and contains 183 poems. However, nothing is known concerning the written source of either of these versions.[17] Malik Fazl Din's 1915 edition has become the basis for most later editions and translations. Several attempts have been made to establish a reliable version of Bahu's Punjabi poetry, the most notable being by Sultan Altaf Ali (who has consulted the greatest number of sources) and Sayyid Nazir Ahmed (who has made an attempt at reconstructing the poems using a literary historical methodology).[18] I have relied on these two editions in preparing my translations of Bahu's work.

Although they are better than all other editions of Bahu's *Abyāt*, both Sultan Altaf Ali's and Sayyid Nazir Ahmed's versions suffer from shortcomings, in large part due to difficulties endemic to the study of Muslim (as opposed to Sikh) Punjabi literature at this point in time. Punjabi has traditionally been seen as an oral language and treated as unworthy of being written down. As a result, the earliest known written examples of Bahu's *Abyāt* date from two centuries after his death; there is, therefore, a certain futility to a text critical method of establishing an accurate version of his Punjabi poetry. It is conceivable that valuable manuscripts of the *Abyāt* are waiting to be discovered in unattended private libraries, but the current written records of the *Abyāt* have no textual connection with Sultan Bahu or his immediate disciples.

Given the complete absence of a manuscript tradition, it would be methodologically more productive to take an oral, folkloric rather than a philological approach to studying not only the *Abyāt* of Bahu but also the entire canon of premodern Punjabi poetry. Bahu's poetry exists, is transmitted, and is appreciated almost entirely as an oral form accompanied by music. Anonymous poets have composed verses that have been attributed to Bahu, and his own verses have been modified in terms of vocabulary, meter, and style to suit the dialects and tastes of the audience. Attempts to recover Bahu's own poems require the establishment not only of a Punjabi grammar, but

16

also a historical grammar of the Doabi Punjabi dialect of two centuries ago. Sayyid Nazir Ahmed's attempt at making the *Abyāt* fit the standards of Urdu and Persian metrics is flawed in precisely this respect. In contrast, Sultan Altaf Ali's methodology of allowing the most popular versions to represent the text seems better, and I have followed him in this regard except when obvious Urdu words have crept into his edition. The literature is oral, and the most widely circulated variants should be considered the most representative.

There are two existing English translations of Sultan Bahu's *Abyāt*. The first and better known one is by Maqbool Elahi.[19] This edition includes the Punjabi text as an appendix, and has useful notes. The second is a partial translation preceded by an uncritical study of Sultan Bahu's life and thought by L. R. Krishna and A. R. Luther.[20] Both translations are somewhat dated in their idiom, and sacrifice accuracy of meaning in favor of rhyme and meter (this is explicitly stated as a goal by Maqbool Elahi). Furthermore, the number of verses in the poems in these translations does not correspond to those in the original *Abyāt*, and the chosen rhyme has no similarity to that of Bahu's work. Both editions are out of print.

NOTES

1. Cf. page 114.
2. Cf. page 56.
3. Cf. page 24.
4. Cf. page 134.
5. Cf. page 89.
6. Cf. page 122.
7. Cf. page 77.
8. Cf. page 42.
9. Cf. page 111.
10. For a discussion of the relationship between this tradition and the Sufi poetry of Sindh, see Ali S. Asani and Kamal Abdel-Malek, *Celebrating Muham-*

mad: Images of the Prophet in Popular Muslim Poetry (Columbia: University of South Carolina Press, 1995), 26ff.

11. Cf. page 75. There is a parallel between this phenomenon and the concept of the church—and therefore its individual members—as the bride of Christ, an idea which is seen frequently in Christian mystical poetry. However, given the fact that the primary cultural contacts between the Christian and Islamic civilizations during this period were through the Mediterranean world and the Middle East, and that this metaphor is not prevalent in the Islamic literature of that area, it is unlikely that the mystic as a bride of God was taken by Indian Sufis from Christianity.

12. There is a substantial body of literature on the language policies of the British in India and of post-partition Pakistan. For information on the history of Punjabi during this period, see C. Shackle, "Language and Cultural Identity in Pakistan Punjab," in Gopal Krishna, ed., *Contributions to South Asian Studies*, vol. 1 (Delhi: Oxford University Press, 1979), 137–60, and "Some Observations on the Evolution of Modern Standard Punjabi," in Joseph T. O'Connell et al., eds., *Sikh History and Religion in the Twentieth Century*, South Asian Studies Papers, no. 3 (Toronto: University of Toronto, Centre for South Asian Studies, 1990), 101–9.

13. The most famous rendition of this story is by the Punjabi poet Waris Shah. It has several English translations; see, for example, Charles F. Usborne, *The Adventures of Hir Ranjha* (London: P. Owen, 1973), and Sayyid Fayyaz Mahmud, *Folk Romances of Pakistan* (Islamabad: Lok Virsa and Sang-e Meel Publications, 1995). The best study of this epic is in Denis Matringe, *Hir Varis Shah: poème panjabi du XVIIIe siècle* (Pondicherry: Institut français, 1988).

14. For an introductory discussion of his Persian works, see Sajidullah Tafhimi, "Shaykh Sultan Bahu: His Life and Persian Works," *Journal of the Pakistan Historical Society* 28:2 (1980), 133–50.

15. Annotated descriptions of these works can be found in Sayyid Ahmad Sa'id Hamadani, *Ahwāl-u maqāmāt-i Hazrat Sultān Bāhū*, edited by Hafiz M. Afzal Faqir (Islamabad: Islamic Book Foundation, 1991).

16. Mas'ud Qurayshi, trans., *Naqsh-i Bāhū: Hazrat Sultān Bāhū kā fārsī kalām awr urdū tarjama* (Islamabad: Lok Virsa, n.d.).

17. A detailed discussion of the various editions of the *Abyāt* is contained in Sayyid Nazir Ahmed, ed., *Kalām-i Sultān Bāhū* (Lahore: Packages Ltd., 1981).

18. Sultan Altaf Ali, ed. and trans., *Abyāt-i Bāhū* (Lahore: Al-Faruq Book Foundation, n.d.).

19. *The "Abyāt" of Sultān Bāhoo* (Lahore: Sh. Muhammad Ashraf, 1967).

20. *Sultan Bahu: Sufi Poet of the Punjab* (Lahore: Sh. Mubarak Ali, 1982).

SULTAN BAHU'S
MYSTICAL POEMS

- body
  - bones
  - cells
  - jugular
- pain, pain-stricken
- power of the mystic guide
- curtains
- seas, floods, water

p 116 - neither Hindu nor Muslim

جتھّے رتی عشق وکاوے اوتھے منّاں ایمان دویے ہو

کتب کتاباں ورد وظیفے اوتر چا کچیوے ہو

باجھوں مرشد کجھ ناں حاصل توڑے راتیں جاگ پڑھیوے ہو

مریئے مرن تھیں اگے باہو تاں رب حاصل تھیوے ہو

Where one gram of love is sold, there one should give tons of faith.

Books, prayers, and liturgies should be heaped on top.

Nothing is gained without a guide, even if one stays up nights

    in study.

Let us die before dying, Bahu, only then is the Lord attained.

دنیــا ڈھـونڈن والے کُتّے در در پھـرن حیــرانی ہو

ہڈی اُتّے ہوڑ تـنھاں دی لـڑدیـاں عـمر وہـانی ہو

عقل دے کوتاہ سمجھـ ناں جانن پیون لوڑن پانی ہو

بـاجھوں ذکـر ربّے دے بـاہـو کوڑی رام کھـانی ہو

Seekers of this world are like dogs, wandering from door to door
in wonder.

Their attention is riveted on a bone, their lives wasted in bickering.

Short on intelligence and unable to understand, they set out in
search of water.

Apart from recollection of the Lord, Bahu, all else is idle chatter.

جو دل مـنگے ہووے نـاہیـں ہوون رہیا پـریرے ہو

دوست ناں دیوے دل دا دارو عشق ناں واگاں پھیرے ہو

اس مـیـدان مـحبّت دے وچ مـلن تـا تکھـیـرے ہو

مـیں قربان تنھاں توں باہو جنھاں رکھیا قدم اگیرے ہو

The heart's desire is unfulfilled and distant.

My Lover won't give it medicine, and it won't mend its ways.

Hotter fires burn in love's battlefield

And, Bahu, I'm in awe of those who charge in.

گُجھے سائے رب صاحب والے کُجھ نہیں خبر اصل دی ہو

گندم دانہ بُہتا چگیا ہن گل پئی ڈور ازل دی ہو

پھاہی دے وچ میں پئی تڑفاں بلبل باغ مثل دی ہو

غیر دلے تھیں سٹ کے باہو رکھیئے امید فضل دی ہو

The hidden shadows of the Lord Master, nothing is known of

    their source.

I pecked and ate many grains of wheat, now the string of eternity

    is around my neck.

I flutter, caught in the noose, like the nightingale in the garden.

Tossing all else from the heart, Bahu, keep hoping for grace.

nightingale: a very common metaphor for the Sufi lover in the courtly tradition
of Persian mystical poetry. The nightingale sings to express its love for the rose,
which sits unattainable in a circle of thorns. In this poem, Bahu carries the
metaphor one step further by implying that the nightingale's love draws it un-
controllably to the rose garden where it becomes trapped in a snare. This con-
cept of being drawn to one's own destruction through love for the beloved is
common in Sufi poetry; it is frequently evoked through the image of a moth
being drawn toward a candle, only to be consumed by the flame.

ایہ تن میرا چشماں ہووے تے میں مرشد ویکھ ناں رجّاں ہو

لوں لوں دے مڈھ لکھ لکھ چشماں ہك کھولاں ہك کجّاں ہو

اتنیاں ڈٹھیِاں صبر ناں آوے ہور کتے ول بھجّاں ہو

مرشد دا دیدار ہے باہو مینوں لکھ کروڑاں حجّاں ہو

Were my body to become one large eye, I would not see enough

   of my guide.

In every cell a million eyes, I'd close one and open another.

Even seeing this much wouldn't calm me, what else can I do?

Bahu, one vision of my guide is as a million billion pilgrimages.

pilgrimage: a reference to the Hajj, the pilgrimage to Mecca that all Muslims are ritually obligated to undertake once in their lifetime if they have the means. The Hajj must be undertaken on the 7th through the 10th days of the last month of the Islamic lunar calendar (this month is called Zu'l-hijja [month of the Hajj] in recognition of the paramount importance of the ritual). A major portion of the pilgrimage consists in circumambulating (*tawāf*) the Ka'ba, a building believed to have been built by the prophet Ibrahim (Abraham) at God's command. All the ritual activities undertaken during the Hajj imitate the actions of the Prophet Muhammad and are believed to commemorate events in the life of Ibrahim and his family. As such, the Hajj is not only a major ritual that enforces God's covenantal relationship with Muslims, but by bringing Muslims together from all parts of the world, it also is a crucial display of Islamic social solidarity. Thus any statement that seems to trivialize the Hajj has enormous impact on a Muslim audience. The classical Sufi figure al-Hallaj (d. 922) is famous for having built a model of the Ka'ba in his house. This action, intended to demonstrate the hollow nature of blindly engaging in rituals without understanding their underlying meaning, scandalized the orthodox establishment of his day. Bahu and (educated) members of his audience were, no doubt, familiar with al-Hallaj's action.

پاک پلیت ناں ہوندے ہرگز توڑے رہندے وچ پلیتی ہو
وحدت دے دریا اچھلے ہک دل صحی ناں کیتی ہو
ہک بت خانیں واصل ہوئے ہک پڑھ پڑھ رہن مسیتی ہو
فاضل سٹ فضیلت بیٹھے باہو عشق نماز جاں نیتی ہو

The pure will never be impure, even if they live in filth.

The seas of unity are crashing near, but one heart hasn't learned

its lesson.

Some attain the goal in idol temples, while others stay glued to

their books in mosques.

Many a scholar tossed scholarship aside, Bahu, when he vowed the

prayer of love.

بـغـداد شہـر دی کیـا نشـانی اُچیـاں لـمیـاں چیـراں ہو

تـن مـن میـرا پـرزے پـرزے جیـوں درزی دیـاں لیـراں ہو

اینھـاں لیـراں دی گل کفنـی پا کے رلـساں سنگ فـقیراں ہو

بغداد شہـر دے ٹکڑے منگـساں باہو کرساں "میراں! میراں!" ہو

I have no souvenirs of Baghdad except wounds, long and deep.

My body and soul have been cut to pieces, like the clippings of
a tailor.

I'll wrap a shroud of these clippings around my neck and join a
group of beggars. _mystics_

I'll beg for Baghdad's scraps, Bahu, and cry out "Miran! Miran!"

Baghdad: 'Abd al-Qadir al-Jilani (d. 1165), after whom the Qadiri Sufi order (to which Bahu belonged) takes its name, is buried in Baghdad. The Qadiri Sufi order is one of the most widely distributed in the Islamic world, and al-Jilani's tomb serves as an important pilgrimage site. Baghdad also holds a special place in the Islamic imagination, because it was the seat of the Caliphate during its heyday.

beggar: the word is _faqir,_ which means both beggar and mystic. Underlying this ambiguity is the common Sufi belief that material poverty is a necessary prerequisite for spiritual wealth.

"Miran!": an epithet of Sultan Bahu's spiritual master.

جیوندے کے جانن سار مویاں دی سو جانے جو مردا ہو

قبراں دے وچ اَن ناں پانی اتھے خرچ لوڑیندا گھردا ہو

ہك وچھوڑا ماں پیو بھائیاں دوجا عذاب قبر دا ہو

واہ نصیب انھانڈا باہو جھڑا وچ حیاتی مردا ہو

What do the living know of the dead? Only they know who die.

The grave has neither food nor water, one must bring supplies

> from home.

Leaving one's mother, father, and brothers, then the torments of

> the grave . . .

How fortunate are they, Bahu, who die while still living!

ناں میں عالم ناں میں فاضل ناں مفتی ناں قاضی ہو

ناں دل میرا دوزخ منگے ناں شوق بہشتیں راضی ہو

ناں میں تریہے روزے رکھے ناں میں پاك نمازی ہو

باجھ وصال اللّه دے باہو دنیا کوڑی بازی ہو

Neither am I a sage, nor am I a scholar, nor a cleric, nor a judge.

Neither does my heart ask for hell, nor is it content with fondness
for paradise.

Neither did I keep the thirty fasts, nor am I a pure, praying person.

Unless you attain Allah, Bahu, this world is but a game.

thirty fasts: a reference to the daily fasts for the entire month of Ramadan.

pure, praying person: praying five times a day and fasting from before sunrise
until after sunset during the entire month of Ramadan are two of the five ritual
requirements of Islam. The other three are the Hajj (see page 25), giving a per-
centage of one's wealth in charity, and striving in the path of God.

ایمان سلامت ہر کوئی منگے عشق سلامت کوئی ہو

منگن ایمان شرماون عشقوں دل نوں غیرت ہوئی ہو

جس منزل نوں عشق پچاوے ایمان نوں خبر ناں کوئی ہو

میرا عشق سلامت رکھیں باہو ایمانوں دیاں دھروئی ہو

Everyone asks for firmness in faith, but few for firmness in love.

They ask for faith and are ashamed of love, such arrogant hearts!

Faith has no idea of the place where love transports you.

I swear by my faith, Bahu, keep my love firm!

کیا ہویا بُت اوڈھر ہویا دل ہرگز دور ناں تھیوے ہو

سے کوہاں میرا مرشد وسدا مینوں وچ حضور دسیوے ہو

جیندے اندر عشق دی رتی اوہ بن شرابوں کھیوے ہو

نام فقیر تنہاں دا باہو قبر جنہاں دی جیوے ہو

So what if love's idol is hidden? One's heart will never be far away.

My guide lives many mountains away, but he is visible before me.

Whoever has one grain of love is drunk without wine.

They are the true mystics, Bahu, whose graves are alive.

idol: in Punjabi, *but,* a term frequently used in Indo-Persian poetry to denote the beloved. This word has striking literary connotations because of the Islamic ban on the construction, possession, or worship of idols or icons in any form.

اللّٰہ صحی کیتوسے جداں چمکیا عشق اگویاں ہو

راتیں دیہاں دیوے تا تکھیرے نت کرے اگویاں سویاں ہو

اندر بھاہیں اندر بالن اندر دے وچ دھویاں ہو

باہو شوہ تداں لدھیوسے جداں عشق کیتوسے سویاں ہو

I knew God well when love flashed before me.

It gives me strength by night and day, and shows what lies ahead.

In me are flames, in me is fuel, in me is smoke.

I only found my Beloved, Bahu, when love made me aware.

ایہو نفس اساڈا بیلی جو نال اساڈیے سدھّا ہو

زاہد عالم آن نوائے جتھّے ٹکڑا ویکھے تھِدھا ہو

جو کوئی اسدی کرے سواری اس نام اللہ دا لدھا ہو

راہ فقر دا مشکل باہو گھر ماں ناں سیرا ردھّا ہو

Only such a soul as my companion that is with me all the way . . .

One that makes strict scholars bow down when they see a scrap
　　of food.

Whoever rides forth upon this soul has learned the name of God.

The mystic path is hard, Bahu, not mother's home cooking!

mystic path: literally, "path of poverty" (see page 27).

اللہ پڑھیوں پڑھ حافظ ہویوں ناں گیا حجابوں پردا ہو

پڑھ پڑھ عالم فاضل ہویوں بھی طالب ہویوں زر دا ہو

سیئے ہزار کتاباں پڑھیاں پر ظالم نفس ناں مردا ہو

باجھ فقیراں کسے ناں ماریا باہو ایہو چور اندر دا ہو

Part of Sufi meditational practice

Repeating "Allah!" you've memorized Him, but the veils have

    not gone.

You've become a learned scholar through constant study, but still

    you seek gold.

You've read thousands of books, but your cruel soul will not die.

Bahu, none but the mystics have killed this inner thief.

---

cruel soul: in Punjabi, *nafs*. In Islamic mystical philosophy and theology the soul is equated with the base, appetitive aspect of a human being, as distinct from the heart (*qalb*) and spirit (*rūh*) which are seen as sources of goodness. The soul is often called *an-nafs al-ʾammāra biʾs-sūʾ* (the soul that incites to evil) and is therefore considered an ally of Satan in his attempts to turn the virtuous believer away from the righteous path. Sufi writings often distinguish between three different souls: the soul that incites to evil (often called the lower soul), the censorious soul (*an-nafs al-lawwāma*), and the contented soul (*an-nafs al-mutmaʾinna*).

اوجھــــڑ جھــــــل تے مــــارو بــــیـــلا جتھـــے جــالـــن آئـــی ہو
جـس کــدھی نــوں ڈھاہ ہمیشاں اوہ ڈھٹھی کـل ڈھائی ہو
نیـں جنھـاندی وِے سراندی اوہ سُکھ نہیـں سونـدے راہی ہو
ریت تے پانی جتھے ہون اکٹھّے باہو اوتھے بنی نہیں بجھدی کائی ہو

Wild marshes and shifting sands are where this life finds itself.

A collapsing riverbank must give way tomorrow if not today.

Those toward whom the river is rising never sleep soundly.

Bahu, you cannot build a dam on sand and water.

christian idea, as well
- good foundation

احـد جـد دتـی وكهـالی از خــود ہویـا فـانی ہو

قرب وصال مقام ناں منزل ناں اوتھے جسم ناں جانی ہو

ناں اوتھے عشق محبّت کائی ناں اوتھے کون مكانی ہو

عینـوں عیـن تھیـوسے باہو سـرّ وحـدت سبحانی ہو

When You made a show of unity, I was lost to myself.

Neither intimacy nor union, stage nor goal, body nor soul remain.

Nor is there love of any kind, nor place, nor being.

In that instant, Bahu, I was faced with the secret of divine unity.

This poem contains a number of technical terms commonly used in Sufi writing that would suggest that a subsection of the audience would be familiar with the philosophical side of Sufism in addition to the message of love and faith which is familiar from Bahu's other poems. Even though the nuances of these terms vary over time (and even from writer to writer), they have shared meanings in Sufi literature: *ahad* (translated as "unity" in the first line) literally means "one." It is a reference to the singularity of God, and immediately brings to mind the first verse of one of the most famous chapters of the Qur'an (Chapter 112). In the same line, *fānī* (translated as "lost") derives from *fanā*, the Sufi concept according to which one of the goals of all mystical exercises is annihilation of the identity of the mystic, whereupon it either dissolves in or is replaced by the greater identity of God. The terms "intimacy" (*qurb*) and "union" (*wisāl*) both refer to stages (*maqām*) on the same quest.

اللہ چمبے دی بوٹی میرے من وچ مرشد لائی ہو

نفی اثبات دا پانی ملیس ہر رگے ہر جائی ہو

اندر بوٹی مشك مچایا جاں پھلاں تے آئی ہو

جیوے مرشد کامل باہو جیں ایہ بوٹی لائی ہو

The guide planted God's jasmine plant within me.

He watered my veins with "negation and affirmation."

Blossoming, the bush spread its fragrance through me.

Long live my perfect guide, Bahu, who has planted this shrub!

---

jasmine plant: in the poem it is the *champa,* a plant bearing fragrant golden flowers.

"negation and affirmation": a name for the Islamic creedal formula "There is no god but God," which negates the existence of false gods before it affirms the existence of the unique true God. This statement is considered one of the most efficacious formulas for Sufi meditation.

ازل ابــد نـوں صحی کیتـوسے ویکھ تمـاشے گزرے ہو

چــوداں طبــق دلینـڈے انــدر آتــش لائے حجـرے ہو

جنہـاں حـق نـاں حاصل کیتا اوہ دوہیں جہـانیں اجـڑے ہو

عاشق غرق ہوے وچ وحدت باہو ویکھ تنہاںڈے مجرے ہو

Having learned the lessons of eternity, we saw spectacles of the past.

Fourteen levels has the heart, where fire has struck up a home.

Those who do not attain the Truth are wretched in both realms.

Lovers drown in divine unity, Bahu, see their incredible end!

levels has the heart: the notion of a spiritual body corresponding to the physical human body is common in Sufism. Bahu is referring to a belief that the heart, as the place or "lens" through which this spiritual body is accessed, has levels of being through which the mystic must progress in order to attain the final goal.

ادھی لعنت دنیاں تائیں تے ساری دنیاں داراں ہو

جیں راہ صاحب دے خرچ ناں کیتی لین غضب دیاں ماراں ہو

پئوواں کولوں پتّر کوہاوے بھٹھ دنیاں مکاراں ہو

جنہاں ترک دنیاں دی کیتی باہو لیسن باغ بہاراں ہو

Half the curses on the world, and all of them on the worldly.

Whoever does not sow in the path of the Lord will reap the lashes

　of torment.

Burn, evil world, which causes fathers to sacrifice their sons!

Those who give up this world, Bahu, will gain gardens in bloom.

sacrifice their sons: this probably alludes to the story of Ibrahim and his willing-
ness to sacrifice his son.

اکھیں سرخ مونہیں تے زردی ہر ولوں دل آہیں ہو
مہا مہاڑ خوشبوئی والا پھونتا ونج کداہیں ہو
عشق مشک ناں چھپے رہندے ظاہر تھیں اتھاہیں ہو
نام فقیر تنھانڈا باہو جنھاں لا مکانی جاہیں ہو

Eyes red, faces pale, rending sighs from every heart . . .

How far away has that perfumed face gone?

Love and musk cannot remain hidden; they must show themselves.

They are the true mystics, Bahu, whose place is "no place."

"no place": *lā makān,* meaning a location beyond the confines of linear time and space.

اندر کلمه کل کل کردا عشق سکھایا کلماں ہو

چوداں طبق کلمے دے اندر قرآن کتاباں علماں ہو

کانے کپ کے قلم بناون لکھ ناں سکن قلماں ہو

باہو ایہہ کلمه مینوں پیر پڑھایا ذرا ناں رہیاں الماں ہو

The creed resounds within me, the creed that love taught me.

Fourteen levels has the creed: the Qur'an, books, all sciences.

They shape reeds into pens, but the pens cannot write it!

Bahu, my master taught me this creed, and now no pain remains.

---

creed: kalma, translated as "creed" throughout this book, refers to the Islamic profession of faith (*al-kalima at-tayyiba*). Uttering the formula "There is no god but Allah, and Muhammad is the messenger of Allah" constitutes the act of conversion to Islam. This statement is believed to have quasi-magical powers, and the first half of it is one of the most common formulas used in Sufi *zikr.*

ایہ تن رب سچّے دا حجرا دل کھّڑیا باغ بہاراں ہو

وچّے کوزے وچّے مصلّے وچّے سجدے دیاں تھاراں ہو

وچّے کعبہ وچّے قـبلہ وچّے الأ اللّہ پکـاراں ہو

کـامـل مرشـد ملیـا بـاہـو اوہ آپے لیسی ساراں ہو

This body is a dwelling of the true Lord, and my heart like a

    garden in bloom.

Within it are fountains, within it are prayer grounds, within it

    places to bow down in prayer.

Within it is the Ka'ba, within it the *qibla,* within it cries of

    "Only Allah!"

I found the Perfect Guide, Bahu, He alone will take care of me.

qibla: the direction toward the Ka'ba, which Muslims face when they pray. It is normally marked by a niche which is one of the main architectural features in a mosque.

Perfect Guide: God is the Perfect Guide who leads Sufis once they have passed the point beyond which a human guide cannot take them.

آپ ناں طالب ہیں کہیں دے لوکاں نوں طالب کردے ہو

چاون کھیپاں کردے سیپاں اللہ دے قہر توں ناہیں ڈردے ہو

عشق مجازی تلکن بازی پیر اولّے دھردے ہو

او شرمندے ہوسن باہو اندر روز حشر دے ہو

They study nothing themselves but make students of others.

They demand oaths of loyalty, not fearing the wrath of God.

Symbolic love is a slippery slope, yet they step upon it.

Bahu, will *they* be ashamed on the Day of Reckoning!

symbolic love: symbolic or metaphorical love (*'ishq-i majāzi*) is the human love of God which is often represented in erotic metaphors. This love, one of the most powerful aspects of Sufi poetry, can also be between two human beings. The most famous instance of this is in the work of Mawlana Jalal ad-din-i Rumi (d. 1273) who dedicated the bulk of his poetry to his friend Shams-i Tabrizi (d. 1248). Symbolic love has very strong homoerotic overtones when applied to love between two human beings, and it is likely that in this poem Bahu is accusing hypocritical Sufi guides and charlatans of engaging in illicit sexual practices.

بـاہـو بـاغ بهـاراں كهـــڑیـاں نـرگــس نـاز شـرم دا ہو
دل وچ کعبہ صحی کیتـو سے پـاکوں پـاك پـرم دا ہو
طـالب طـلـب طـواف تمـامی حبّ حضــور حـرم دا ہو
گیا حجاب تهیوسے حاجی باہو جداں بخشیوس راہ کرم دا ہو

A garden has bloomed, Bahu, shaming the narcissus and the rue.

In my heart I made the Ka'ba out of love.

Seeker, quest, and pilgrimage, all devoted to love of the sacred
    precinct.

The vein vanished, you became a Haji, Bahu, when you were
    blessed with God's bounteous path.

Haji: circumambulation of the Ka'ba is a major part of the Hajj pilgrimage, at
the conclusion of which the pilgrim is known as a Haji.

بـغـداد شـریـف ونـج کـراہـاں سـودانے کتـوسے ہو

رتی عقـل دی کراہاں بھـار غمانْدا گھدوسے ہو

بھـار بھریـرا منزل چوکھیـری اوڑك ونـج پہتیوسے ہو

ذات صفات صحی کتوسے باہو تاں جمال لدھوسے ہو

On going to Baghdad I struck a deal:

For a gram of intellect I took a load of sorrows.

The load grew heavier and my goal more distant, but finally I

   reached it.

It was when I understood essence and attribute, Bahu, that I found

   divine beauty.

essence and attribute: a reference to the distinction between the divine essence
(*zāt*) and attributes (*sifāt*), which is a major topic of discussion not only in
Sufism but also in all schools of Islamic theology. The most widely held under-
standing of this relationship is that God's essence is unchanging and rationally
incomprehensible and that therefore God makes Himself known to human be-
ings through attributes. These attributes are of two types, "intransitive" ones
that simply describe God (e.g., Unique, Eternal) and "transitive" ones that de-
scribe God's relationship to Creation (e.g., Nurturing, Merciful, Wrathful).
The divine attributes are often paired together in stereotypically male and fe-
male pairs to emphasize the fact that God simultaneously encompasses and lies
beyond all qualities (e.g., divine beauty [*jamāl*], mentioned in the final verse, is
a feminine attribute normally paired with divine majesty [*jalāl*], a masculine
attribute). Sufis try to approach God by working to understand His attributes.

بنھ چلایا طرف زمیں دے عرشوں فرش ٹکایا ہو
گھر تیں ملیا دیس نکالا اساں لکھیا جھولی پایا ہو
رہ نی دنیاں ناں کر جھیڑا ساڈا اگے دل گھبرایا ہو
اسیں پردیسی ساڈا وطن دوراڈھا باہو دم دم غم سوایا ہو

I was shackled and marched to the earth—from the heavens

thrown on the ground.

I was exiled from my home, my lap filled with what was fated.

Stop, world! Stop bothering me! My heart is already unsettled.

I am in exile, my home far away, Bahu, and my grief grows with

every breath.

پڑھ پڑھ علم ملوك رجھاون کیا ہویا اس پڑھیاں ہو

ہرگز مکھّن مول ناں آوے پھٹّے دُدھ دے کڑیاں ہو

آکھ چنڈورا ہتھ کے آئیو ایس انگوری چنیاں ہو

ہك دل خستہ رکھیں راضی باہو لہیں عبادت ورہیاں ہو

Through study and learning they earn the pleasure of princes—

what comes of such learning?

Butter never rises from boiling sour milk.

Speak, bird! What do you gain by pecking newly sprouted grain?

Nursing one broken heart, Bahu, is equal to the worship of

many years.

پڑھ پڑھ علم ہزار کتاباں عالم ہوئے بھارے ہو
ہک حرف عشق دا پڑھن ناں جانن بھُلے پھرن وچارے ہو
ہک نگاہ جے عاشق ویکھے لکھ ہزاراں تارے ہو
لکھ نگاہ جے عالم ویکھے کسے ناں کدھی چاہڑے ہو
عشق عقل وچ منزل بھاری سئیاں کوہانٔدے پائے ہو
جنہاں عشق خرید ناں کیتا باہو اوہ دوہیں جہانیں مارے ہو

Having learned wisdom from a thousand books, they become
  great scholars.

They cannot learn one letter of love—the wretches wander in
  ignorance.

If a lover glances just once, he can swim a hundred million rivers.

If the scholar looks a hundred million times, he cannot reach the
  other bank.

Between learning and love is an arduous journey, with many miles
  of distance.

Whoever does not gain love, Bahu, is a loser in both worlds.

48

تُوڑے تنگ پرانے ہوون گجھے ناں رِہندے تازی ہو
مار نقارہ دَل وچ وڑیا کھیڈ گیا ہک بازی ہو
مار دِلاں نوں جوڈ دتونیں جدوں تکے نین نیازی ہو
انہاں نال کیہ ہویا باہو جنہاں یار ناں رکھیا راضی ہو

Arabian stallions cannot be hidden beneath threadbare saddles.

He entered the field striking the drum and played one round.

Strike their hearts and shake them up when they see Your

    beloved eyes.

Bahu, what became of those who did not satisfy their Beloved?

تُوں تاں جاگ ناں جاگ فقیرا انت نوں لوڑ جگایا ہو
اکھیں میٹیاں ناں دل جاگے ، جاگے جاں مطلب پایا ہو
ایہ نقطہ جداں کیتا پختہ تاں ظاہر آکھ سنایا ہو
میں تاں بھلی ویندی ساں باہو مینوں مرشد راہ دکھایا ہو

Wake up or don't, mystic, you'll be awakened by need in the end.

The heart doesn't awaken by closing one's eyes, but only when one
finds the meaning.

When I truly grasped this point, then did I declare it openly:

I was going along mindlessly, Bahu, then the guide showed me
the way.

تسبیح پھری تے دل نہیں پھریا کی لیناں تسبیح پھڑ کے ہو
علم پڑھیا تے ادب ناں سکھیا کی لیناں علم نوں پڑھ کے ہو
چلّے کٹّے تے کجھ ناں کھٹیا کی لیناں چلیاں وڑ کے ہو
جاگ بناں دُدھ جمدے ناہیں باہو بھانویں لال ہونوں کڑھ کڑھ کے ہو

The rosary spun but the heart did not spin, what's the point of

    holding a rosary?

You learned all the sciences but you didn't learn manners; what's

    the point of learning sciences?

You sat for long vigils but experienced nothing, what's the point of

    doing vigils?

Yogurt doesn't set without starter, Bahu, even if you boil milk until

    it browns.

rosary: prayer beads (*tasbīh*) are widely used by Muslims in general and Sufis in particular as an aid to meditation. The most common formulas recited using these beads are "Praise be to God" (*al-hamdu li'llāh*), "God is Great" (*Allāhu akbar*), and "Glory be to God" (*subhān Allāh*). The beads take their Arabic name from the last of these, *tasbīh* being a verbal noun meaning glorification. The formulas are normally recited ninety-nine times or in multiples thereof. For this reason, Islamic rosaries normally have thirty-three or ninety-nine beads.

ثابت عشق تنہاں نیں لدھا جنہاں ترٹی چوڑچا کیتی ہو

ناں اوہ صوفی ناں اوہ صافی ناں سجدہ کرن مسیتی ہو

خالص نیل پرانے اُتّے نہیں چڑھدا رنگ مجیٹھی ہو

قاضی آن شرع ول باہو کدیں عشق نماز ناں نیتی ہو

Those who destroy their own treasures are the ones who find

 true love. *who are they?*

They are not Sufis or ascetics, nor do they bow down inside

 the mosque.

new? Green dye cannot cover pure, old, indigo blue.

Let the judges come to the true law, Bahu, those who have never

 vowed the prayer of love.

lost treasure

جیں دل عشق خرید ناں کیتا سو دل درد ناں پھنّی ہو

اس دل تھیس سنگ پتھر چنگے جو دل غفلت آئی ہو

جیں دل عشق حضور ناں منگیا سو درگاہوں سَٹّی ہو

ملیا دوست ناں انہاں باہو جنہاں چوڑ ناں کیتی تَرَئّی ہو

Pain does not blossom in a heart that has no love.

Rocks and stones are better than a heart mired in ignorance.

A heart that does not ask for love is thrown from the

   divine presence.

Those who do not lose their treasures, Bahu, do not find

   the Friend.

lose treasure

جـنـگـل دے وچ شیـر مـریـلا بـاز پـوے وچ گھـر دے ہو
عـشق جیہا صرّاف نـاں کوئی کجھ نـاں چھوڑے وچ زر دے ہو
عـاشقاں نـیـندر بھـك نـاں کـائی عـاشق مول نـاں مـردے ہو
عـاشق جیندے تڈاں ڈٹھوسے باہو جداں صاحب اگّے سر دھردے ہو

The tiger kills in the jungle, but the falcon even strikes at home.

There is no smith like love, which leaves nothing mixed in

the gold.

pure

Lovers feel neither sleep nor hunger; lovers never die.

We see lovers truly alive, Bahu, when they offer their heads to

the Master.

*death
vs.
life*

جے رب ناتیاں دھوتیاں ملدا تاں ملدا ڈڈواں مچھیاں ہو

جے رب لمیاں والاں ملدا تاں ملدا بھیڈاں سسّیاں ہو

جے رب راتیں جاگیاں ملدا تاں ملدا کال کڑچھیاں ہو

جے رب جتیاں ستیاں ملدا تاں ملدا ڈانداں خصیاں ہو

رب انھاں نوں ملدا باہو نیّتاں جنھاں دیاں اچھیاں ہو

criticizing strict patterns

If the Lord were found by bathing and washing, He would be
found by frogs and fish. *Brahamans*

If the Lord were found by having long hair, He would be found by
sheep and goats. *Yogis*

If the Lord were found by staying awake all night, He would be
found by the cuckoo. *???*

If the Lord were found by being celibate, He would be found by
gelded oxen. *Yogis some Sufis*

The Lord is only found by those, Bahu, whose intentions are good.

publicly tell people you have religion

جنہاں شوہ الف تھیں پایا پھول قرآن ناں پڑھدے ہو
اوہ مـــــارن دم مـــحبّت والا دُور ہـویـونیـں پـردے ہو
دوزخ بـہشـت غـلام تـنہـانڈے چا کیـتونے بـردے ہو
میں قربان تنہاں دے باہو جہڑے وحدت دے وچ وڑدے ہو

Those who find the Beloved in the letter *alif* need not open the

Qur'an to read it.

When they blow with the breath of love, the curtains are

pushed aside.

Heaven and hell are their slaves, made to serve them.

I give my life for those, Bahu, who enter the state of unity.

alif: the first letter of the Arabic alphabet; it is also the first letter of the word "Allah." The letter is a vertical line, identical to the number "one," and is often seen as a symbol of God's unity. In popular Sufism, it is widely believed that truly understanding this letter is equal to the knowledge gained from reading all the books in the world.

جے کر دین علم وچ ہونْدا تاں سر نیزے کیوں چڑھدے ہو

اٹھاراں ہزار جو عالم آیا اوہ اگّے حسین دے مردے ہو

جے کجھ ملاحظہ سرور دا کردے تاں خیمے تمبو کیوں سڑدے ہو

جے کر مندے بیعت رسولی تاں پانی کیوں بند کردے ہو

پر صادق دین تنہاں دے باہو جو سر قربانی کردے ہو

If religion lay in learning, why would they stick their heads

    on lances?

If eighteen thousand sages were there, surely they would have died

    before Husayn!

If they had truly copied the Prophet, then why did the tents burn?

If they had accepted the Messenger's successor, why did they cut

    off the water?

But true religion is theirs, Bahu, who sacrifice their own heads.

This poem alludes to the martyrdom of the Prophet's grandson, Husayn, who,
along with his family, was massacred by troops loyal to the counter-Caliph,
Yazid ibn Muʿawiya, at Karbala in 680 C.E. According to legend, there were
eighteen thousand Muslim sages in the world at that time, none of whom came
to Husayn's aid. Husayn and his family were besieged at Karbala where the en-
emy cut off their water supply to force them to surrender. The siege ended with
the massacre of the majority of males, including Husayn.

چڑھ چنّاں تے کر رشنائی تارے ذکر کریندے تیرا ہو

تیرے جہے چن کئی سے چڑھدے سانوں سجناں باجھ ہنیرا ہو

جتھے چن اساڈا چڑھدا اُتھے قدر نہیں کجھ تیرا ہو

جس دے کارن اساں جنم گوایا باہو یار ملے ہک پھیرا ہو

Arise and shine bright, moon! The stars are engaged in your
recollection.

Many moons like you have risen, but without my Beloved all is
darkness.

scholar?

Where my Moon rises, there you have no worth.

The Beloved for whom I lost a lifetime, may I meet Him just
once, Bahu.

حـافظ پـڑھ پـڑھ کـرن تـکبّـر مُلّاں کـرن وڈیـائـی ہو
سـاون مـاہ دے بـدلاں وانـگوں پھـرن کتـابـاں چـائـی ہو
جتھـے ویکھیـں چنـگا چوکھـا پـڑھـن کلام سـوائـی ہو
دوہیـں جھـانیـں مُٹھـے بـاہو جنھـاں کھـادی ویچ کمـائـی ہو

Qur'an scholars read and aggrandize themselves, priests act

    sanctimonious.

Like rain clouds in the monsoon, they wander heavy with books.

They recite more wherever they see greater gain and plenty.

Bahu, those who sell and eat up their earnings lose both worlds.

خام کیہ جانن سار فقر دی جہڑے محرم ناہیں دل دے ہو

آب مٹی تھیں پیدا ہوئے خامی بھانڈے گل دے ہو

لعل جواہراں دا قدر کی جانن جو سوداگر بل دے ہو

ایمان سلامت سوئی ویسن باہو جہڑے بھج فقیراں ملدے ہو

What do the unfit know, those who do not share the

    heart's secrets?

They are as unbaked clay pots, made from mud and water.

What do merchants of glass know about diamonds and rubies?

Only they shall leave this world with perfect faith, Bahu, who run

    to meet *faqirs*.   beggar/mystic

faqir: literally, "beggar," a common term for a Sufi mystic, suggesting a direct
relationship between spiritual wealth and material poverty.

دل دریا سمندروں ڈونگھے کون دلاں دیاں جانے ہو

وچّے بیڑے وچّے جھیڑے وچّے ونجھ مُہانے ہو

چوداں طبق دلے دے اندر جتھے عشق تنبو ونج تانے ہو

جو دل دا محرم ہووے باہو سوئی رب پچھانے ہو

The heart is deeper than rivers and oceans, who knows what lies
in the heart?

Within it are boats, within it oars, within it boat-poles and
boatmen.

Fourteen levels has the heart, where love has pitched its tent.

Those who are the heart's confidants, Bahu, only they
recognize the Lord.

Fourteen levels has the heart: see p. 38.

progression to goal)

دل کالے کنوں منہ کالا چنگا جے کوئی اس نوں جانے ہو

منہ کالا دل اچھا ہووے تاں دل یار پچھانے ہو

ایہہ دل یار دے پچھے ہووے متاں یار وی کدی پچھانے ہو

سَے عالم چھوڑ مسیتاں نٹھے باہو جد لگے نیس دل ٹکانے ہو

A blackened face is better than a blackened heart, if someone were

to understand this.

Blackened face, good heart—that is how the heart knows

the Beloved.

If such a heart pursues the Beloved, then maybe the Beloved would

know it as well.

Scores of scholars fled the mosque, Bahu, when their hearts were

set aright.

درد اندر دا اندر سازے باہر کراں تاں گھائل ہو

حال اساڈا کیوں اوہ جانن جو دنیا تے مائل ہو

بحر سمندر عشقے والا ہر دم رہندا حائل ہو

پہنچ حضور آسان ناں باہو اساں نام ترے دے سائل ہو

My inner pain burns me inside, and if I bring it out it wounds me.

How can those inclined to this world know the state I'm in?

The ocean of love is always an obstacle:

Reaching the divine presence is not easy, Bahu, so we are asking

Your name. *mystery*

Your name: God is considered to have many names in Islam, the greatest of which is a mystery. It is believed that anyone who knows this name understands the nature of God.

درد منداں دے دھوئیں دھُکھدے ڈردا کوئی ناں سیکے ہو

انھاں دھوئیاں دے تا تکھیرے محرم ہووے تاں سیکے ہو

چھک شمشیر کھڑاہے سر تے ترس پَوَس تاں تھیکے ہو

ساہورے کُڑیئے اپنے وجناں باہو سدا ناں رہناں پیکے ہو

Smoke rises from the painstricken, but no one warms themselves
out of fear.

The heat of this smoke is intense, one could warm oneself if one
knew the secret.   w/pain - smoke

Sword drawn, He stands over my head; He might sheath it if He
feels pity.

Girl, you have to go to your in-laws; you cannot stay with your
parents forever, Bahu.

?? must get married?

64

درد منــداں دا خــون جــو پيــنــدا بــربــوں بــاز مــريـلا هو

چهــاتی دے وچ كيـتُس ڈيـرا جيوں شيــر بيٹهــا مـل بيلا هو

هاتهــی مـسـت سنــدوری وانــگوں كــردا پيــلا پيلا هو

اس پيلے دا وساس ناں كيجے باهو پيلے ناں هوندا ميلا هو

The love which drinks the blood of the painstricken is a deadly

falcon.

It has created a lair in the breast, like the tiger takes over the forest.

Like an elephant drunk on vermilion, it charges and charges.

Do not fear this charge, Bahu, for without the charge there is

no meeting.

love drinks blood of the pain stricken

دین تے دنیا سکیاں بَهیناں تینوں عقل نہیں سمجھیندا ہو

دونْویں اکس نکاح وچ آون تینوں شرع نہیں فرمیندا ہو

جیویں اگ تے پانی تھاں اِکے وچ واسا نہیں کریندا ہو

دوہیں جہانیں مُٹھا باہو جیڑا دعوا کوڑ کریندا ہو

Religion and this world are blood sisters—intellect did not teach

you this.

That both should be betrothed to one person—the law does not

permit this,

Just like fire and water which cannot stay in one vessel.

He is deprived of both worlds, Bahu, who makes false oaths.

دُدھ تے دہی ہر کوئی رڑکے عاشق بھا رڑکیندے ہو
تن چِتُّورا من مندھانی آہیں نال ہلیندے ہو
دکھاں دا نتیرا کڈھے لسکارے غماں دا پانی پَیندے ہو
نام فقیر تنہاں دا باہو جیہڑے ہڈاں توں مکھن کڈھیندے ہو

Everyone churns milk and yogurt, lovers churn fire.

The body the pot, the spirit the churn, they stir it with sighs.

Pulling the strap of heartache, they add the sparkling water

    of sorrow.

They are the true mystics, Bahu, who draw out butter from bones.

*pain

درد منداں دیاں آہیں کولوں پہاڑ پتھر دے جھڑدے ہو

درد منداں دیاں آہیں کولوں بھج نانگ زمیں وچ وڑدے ہو

درد منداں دیاں آہیں کولوں آسمانوں تارے جھڑدے ہو

درد منداں دیاں آہیں کولوں باہو عاشق مول ناں ڈردے ہو

From the sighs of the painstricken, stone mountains fall down.

From the sighs of the painstricken, snakes hurry underground.

From the sighs of the painstricken, stars fall down from

   the heavens.

From the sighs of the painstricken, Bahu, lovers are never afraid.

دل بــازار تـے مــنّـہ دروازہ ســینہ شــہـر ڈسـینـدا ہو

روح سوداگر نفس ہــے راہزن جھڑا حق دا راہ مریندا ہو

جاں توڑی ایـہ نفس ناں ماریں تاں ایـہ وقت کھڑیندا ہو

کـر دا ہــے ضائعا ویلا بـاہـو جـان نــوں تاك مریندا ہو

The heart a bazaar and the mouth a gateway, the breast

  appears as a city.

The spirit a merchant, the soul a robber, who attacks on the

  path of Truth.

As long as you do not kill this soul, your time is being wasted.

It wastes time, Bahu, and puts a padlock on life.

راہ فقـــر دا پــرے پــربــرے اوڑك كــوئـی نــاں دسّـے ہو

ناں اُتھے علم ناں پڑھن پڑھاون ناں اُتھے مسئلے قصّے ہو

ایـہ دنیـا ہے بت پرستی مت کوئی اس تے وِسّے ہو

مـوت فـقیـری جیں سر آوے باہو معلم تھیــوے تسّے ہو

The path of poverty is very long, with no end in sight.

There is neither teaching and learning on it, nor are there issues
   and fables.

This world is idol worship, let no one put any trust in it.

Only they know it, Bahu, on whom befalls the death of poverty.

path of poverty: synonymous with the mystical path.

death of poverty: this could also refer to mystical death or the annihilation of self-
identity toward the end of the Sufi path.

راتیـــں رتی نـندر نــاں آوے دیٹھـاں رہے حـیرانی ہو

عـارف دی گـل عـارف جـانے کیـا جـانے نـفسـانی ہو

کـر عبـادت پـچھوتاسـیں تـیری ضائـعا گئی جوانی ہو

حق حضور اُنهاں نوں حاصل باہو جنهاں ملیا شاہ جیلانی ہو

Not a bit of sleep comes at night and amazement lasts all day.

Only a mystic understands a mystic's words, what do the

  bestial know?

Be busy with worship or else you'll regret the youth you wasted.

The presence of Truth is obtained, Bahu, by those who have met

  the King of Jilan. — *traveled to shrine*

mystic: the term *'ārif* is often translated as "gnostic," although the English term implies a degree of elitism much greater and a variety of knowledge much more arcane than the direct experiential form of knowledge Bahu and poets like him talk about.

King of Jilan: a reference to the Sufi master 'Abd al-Qadir al-Jilani (d. 1165), the eponymous founder of the Qadiri Sufi order to which Sultan Bahu belonged. 'Abd al-Qadir al-Jilani's tomb in Baghdad is a major pilgrimage site and, most probably, Bahu's references to the city of Baghdad and his experiences there refer to his spiritual or imaginary visits to this saint's shrine.

رات اندھیری کالی دے وچ عشق چراغ جلاندا ہو

جیندی سک توں دل چا نیوے توڑیں نہیں آواز سناندا ہو

اوجھڑ جھل تے مارو بیلے اتھے دم دم خوف شیہاں دا ہو

تھل جل جنگل گئے جھگیندے باہو کامل نینہ جنہاندا ہو

On a dark, black night, love lights a lamp.

You can't hear the voice of the One whose love carries your

heart away.

Forests, marshes, and frightening swamps, where one fears tigers

with every breath.

Those whose love is perfect, Bahu, cross deserts, seas, and jungles.

راتیں نین رت ہنجوں روون تے دِہاں غمزہ غم دا ہو

پڑھ توحید وڑیا تن اندر سُکھ آرام ناں سمدا ہو

سر سولی تے چا ٹنگیونیں ایہو راز پرم دا ہو

سدّھا ہو کو ہیوے باہو قطرہ رہے ناں غم دا ہو

At night eyes cry tears of blood and by day shed glances of grief.

When I recited the creed it filled my body, but I cannot sleep
   in peace.

They hung his head on the gallows, such is the secret of love.

Let us head straight to Him, Bahu, not a drop of grief will remain.

creed: in Punjabi, *tawhīd,* which means the formal affirmation of God's unity, usually done by reciting the first half of the Islamic profession of faith.

they hung his head on the gallows: a reference to al-Husayn ibn Mansur al-Hallaj (d. 922), a famous Sufi figure who, according to popular legend, was martyred for publicly declaring his unity with God.

رحمت اس گھر وچ وسّے جتھے بلدے دیوے ہو

عشق ہوائی چڑھ گیا فلک تے کتھے جہاز گھتیوے ہو

عقل فکر دی بیڑی نوں چا پہلے پور بوڑیوے ہو

ہرجا جانی دسّے باہو جتھول نظر کجیوے ہو

Mercy only resides in a house with a burning lamp.

Love sailed into the heavens, where will this ship drop anchor?

One should sink the boat of intellect and rationality on its first trip.

The Beloved is visible everywhere, Bahu, wherever my gaze turns.

زبانی کلمه ہر کوئی پڑھدا دل دا پڑھدا کوئی ہو

جتھے کلمہ دل دا پڑھیئے اتھے ملے زبان ناں ڈھوئی ہو

دل دا کلمہ عاشق پڑھدے کی جانن یار گلوئی ہو

ایہہ کلمہ اسانوں پیر پڑھایا باہو میں سدا سوہاگن ہوئی ہو

Everyone recites the creed of the tongue, few say the creed of
the heart.

Where the creed of the heart is said, there is no room for
the tongue.

The lovers say the creed of the heart, what do sophists know?

It is this creed that the master taught us, Bahu, and now I am
eternally blessed. *Eternal wifehood*

---

eternally blessed: literally, a wife who never becomes a widow; someone in an
eternal state of wifehood. This term is sometimes applied to a particular variety
of Sufi figures in India who dressed as women to symbolize their relationship
with God.) ? ?

زاهــد زهــد کــرینْدے تهــکے روزے نــفــل نمــازاں ہو

عــاشق غرق ہوئے وچ وحدت اللّه نال محبّت رازاں ہو

مکهی قیـد شهـد وچ ہوئی کیا اڈسی نال شاہبازاں ہو

جنهاں مجلس نال نبی دے باہو سوئی صاحب راز نیازاں ہو

Ascetics practice asceticism, exhausted by fasts and excess prayers.

The lovers have drowned in the Unity, now exchanging love and

secrets with God.

The bee is trapped in honey, how can it fly with the falcon?

Only those who sat with the Prophet, Bahu, can offer true prayers.

سـوز کنوں تـن سڑیـا سـارا مـیـں تـے دُکھّـاں ڈیـرے لائـے ہو
کـوئـل وانـگ کـوکیـنـدی وتـاں نـاں وِنجـن دن اضـائـعـے ہو
بـول پپیـہا رُت ساوِن آئـی متـاں مـولا مـیـنـہ ورسائـے ہو
ثابت صدق تـے قدم اگـوِیاں باہو رب سکدیاں دوست ملائـے ہو

My whole body is burned by words, pain has taken me over.

I wander lamenting like the cuckoo, begging that my days not go

by in waste. *(what is my beloved?)*

Speak, bird! The monsoon has come; perhaps God will shed

some rain.

Be sincere and step forward, Bahu, for perhaps the Lord will let the

seekers meet a Friend. *(a spiritual guide?)*

cuckoo: the cuckoo's call is traditionally rendered as the lament "Where has my beloved gone?" Another interpretation is that the cuckoo is repeating "Hu! Hu!" ("Him! Him!" a reference to God). In both cases the cuckoo serves as a metaphor for the mystic's soul. For more information on the importance of birds in Sufi literature, see pp. 5–6.

سُن فریاد پیراں دیا پیرا میں آکھ سناواں کینوں ہو
تیرے جیہا مینوں ہور ناں کوئی میں جیہاں لکھ تینوں ہو
پھول ناں کاغذ بدیاں والے در توں دھک ناں مینوں ہو
میں وچ ایڈ گناہ ناں ہوندے باہو توں بخشیندوں کینوں ہو

Hear my request, master of masters! Who else can I address

out loud?

There is no one else like you for me—like me there are a hundred

thousand for you.

Do not open the register of wrongs! Do not push me out the door!

If there were not so many sins in me, Bahu, whom would

you absolve?

سینے وچ مقام ہے کیندا سانوں مرشد گل سمجھائی ہو

ایہو ساہ جو آوے جاوے ہور نہیں شے کائی ہو

اس نوں اسم الاعظم آکھن ایہو سرّ الہی ہو

ایہو موت حیاتی باہو ایہو بھیت الہی ہو

"Whose place is in the breast?" The guide made us understand

    these words.

This very breath that comes and goes—there is nothing besides it.

They call this the Greatest Name; this is the divine mystery. *[name of God]*

This is the living death, Bahu, this is the divine secret.

---

divine mystery: the greatest name of God (*al-ism al-a'zam*) is unknown, its nature
being the divine mystery.

شور شہر تے رحمت وسّے جتھے باہو جالے ہو
باغباں دے بوئے وانگوں طالب نت سمبھالے ہو
نال نظارے رحمت والے کھڑا حضوروں پالے ہو
ناں فقیر تنہاں دا باہو جہڑا گھر وچ یار وکھا لے ہو

May mercy rain on the wretched town where Bahu lives.

He guards the seeker as a gardener guards his plants.

With glances of mercy, He nurtures with the Presence.

Bahu, the true mystic is one who can see the Beloved

    while at home.

شـــريعـــت دے دروازے اُچّے راہ فــقــر دا مـــوری ہو
عالم فاضل لنگھن ناں دیندے جو لنگھدا سو چوری ہو
پُٹ پُٹ اِنّـاں وئّے مـارن دردمنداں دے کھـــوری ہو
راز ماہی دا عاشق جانن باہو کی جانن لوک اتھوری ہو

The gates of the law are high, the mystic path a tiny doorway.

Sages and scholars let no one pass; whoever succeeds does so

    in secret.

Those who bear the painstricken malice, dig up and throw bricks

    and stones.

Only the lovers know the Beloved's secret, Bahu, what do donkey

    drovers know?

[handwritten annotations:] Scholars? uneducated? they can't be lovers?

[handwritten:] tiny door? but for mystics

صورت نفس امّارہ دی کوئی کُتّا گُلّر کالا ہو

کوکے نوکے لہو پیوے منگے چرب نوالا ہو

کھبّے پاسوں اندر بیٹھا دل دے نال سنبھالا ہو

ایہ بدبخت ہے وڈا ظالم باہو کرسی اللہ ٹالا ہو

The appearance of the inciting soul is like some black cur or its
offspring.

It barks and howls, drinks blood, and asks for a soft morsel.

It sits comfortably on the left side, next to the heart.

This ill-omened one is the great tormentor, Bahu, God guard
us from it!

ظاهر ویکھاں جانی تائیں نالے دسّے اندر سینے ہو

بربوں ماری میں نت پھراں مینوں ہسّ لوك نابینے ہو

میں دل وچّوں ہے شوہ پایا لوك جاوِن مکّے مدینے ہو

کہے فقیر میراں دا باہو سب دلانْدے وچ خزینے ہو

I see my Lover on the outside, and He is also visible in my breast.

I wander lovestruck; the blind laugh at me.

I found the Beloved in my heart, while others search in Mecca
and Medina.

The mystic of Miran says, "Bahu, all treasures are in the heart."

Medina: the city where the Prophet Muhammad settled after he was expelled
from his birthplace of Mecca. Because he is buried in Medina that city has be-
come a major Islamic pilgrimage site and is frequently visited as an extension of
the Hajj pilgrimage.

mystic of Miran: a reference to 'Abd al-Qadir al-Jilani to whose Sufi order Bahu
belonged.

علموں باجھوں فقر کماوے کافر مرے دیوانہ ہو

سے وربیانڈی کرے عبادت رہے اللہ کنوں بیگانہ ہو

غفلت کنوں ناں کھلسن پردے دل جاہل بتخانہ ہو

میں قربان تنہاں توں باہو جنہاں ملیا یار یگانہ ہو

mysticism?

Whoever strives for poverty without knowledge dies a heretic
and insane.

He does acts of worship for years but remains ignorant of Allah.

The curtains do not open through heedlessness; his heart is a
benighted idol temple.

My life goes to those, Bahu, who have met the Singular Friend.

God is a friend

عقل فکر دی جا ناں کائی جتھے وحدت سرّ سبحانی ہو

ناں اوتھے مُلّاں پنڈت جوشی ناں اوتھے علم قرآنی ہو

جد احمد احد وکھالی دتّا تاں کُلّ ہووے فانی ہو

علم تمام کیتونیں حاصل باہو کتاباں ٹھپ آسمانی ہو

There is no room for rationality where there is the glorious

  mystery of divine unity,

Here there are neither mullahs, pandits, and astrologers, nor the

  outward meaning of the Qur'an.

When Ahmad appears as the One, all else is destroyed.

Perfect knowledge is obtained, Bahu, by those who close the

  revealed scriptures.

outward meaning of the Qur'an: the Qur'an is believed by Sufis to have two
dimensions, an exoteric, literal one which is apparent to anyone who can read
the words, and an esoteric, symbolic one, which is only known to those who
possess a high level of mystical attainment. "Mullah" is a term for an Islamic
cleric and "pandit" for a Hindu priest; both are frequently used by Bahu with
derogatory connotations.

Ahmad: another name for the Prophet Muhammad.

عاشق ہونویں تے عشق کمانویں دل رکھیں وانگ پہاڑاں ہو

لکھ لکھ بدیاں تے ہزار اُلاہمے کر جانیں باغ بہاراں ہو

منصور جیہے چُك سولی دتّے جیہڑے واقف کل اسراراں ہو

سجدیوں سر ناں چائیے باہو توڑے کافر کہن ہزاراں ہو

If you want to be a lover and earn love, then make your heart like
the mountains.

Consider hundreds of thousands of acts of enmity and hundreds of
calumnies to be gardens in bloom.

Like Mansur, those privy to all secrets were hung from the gallows.

Do not raise your head from prostration, Bahu, even if thousands
call you an infidel.

Mansur: another allusion to the Sufi martyr, al-Husayn ibn Mansur al-Hallaj.

عــاشق راز ماہی دے کولوں کدی ناں ہوون وانڈے ہو

نیندر حرام تنہاں تے ہوئی جہڑے اسم ذات کمانڈے ہو

ہك پل مول آرام ناں کردے دینہہ رات وتن کرُلانڈے ہو

جنہاں الف صحی کر پڑھیا باہو واہ نصیب تنہانڈے ہو

Lovers are never free from the mysteries of the Beloved.

Sleep is forbidden to those who obtain the name of the Essence.

They do not rest for a single instant, wandering in lamentation

day and night.

What good fortune is theirs, Bahu, who have learned the *alif*

correctly!

[handwritten: to know is to lament?]

learned the alif: see p. 56.

عـاشق عـشق مـاہی دے کولوں نت پھرن ہمیـشاں کھیـوے ہو
جنہاں جیندیاں جان ماہی نوں دتّی اوہ دوہیں جھانیں جیوے ہو
شـمـع چـراغ جـنہاں دل روشـن اوہ کیـوں بـالـن ڈیوے ہو
عقل فکر دی پہنچ ناں کائی باہو اوتھے فانی فہم کچیوے ہو

Lovers always wander drunken from their love of the Beloved.

Those who give the Beloved their lives while still living are alive

in both worlds.

Those in whose hearts lamps are shining, why should they

light candles?

Intellect and rationality have no reach there, Bahu, such

understanding should be destroyed.

destroyed: the word used here for destruction is a technical Sufi term mean-
ing the annihilation of all self-consciousness, which is then replaced by divine
consciousness.

عـــاشـــق دا دل مــوم بـرابـــر مـعـشـوقـاں وَل کــالــی ہو
طـامـاں ویکھے تُرتُر تـگّے جیـوں بـازاں دے چـالی ہو
بـــاز وچـــارہ کـنـونْکر اُڈے پَیـریں پـیـوس دوالــی ہو
جیں دل عشق خرید ناں کیتا باہو دوہاں جہانوں خالی ہو

A lover's heart is like melted wax, rushing toward its beloved.

Seeing prey, it stares greedily, as is the habit of hawks.

How can the poor falcon fly, for its feet have been bound.

Whoever does not possess love, Bahu, loses both worlds.

عـاشقاں ہکو وضـو جـو کیتا روز قیـامت تـائیں ہو

وچ نمـاز رکوع سـجودے رہـندے سـنـج صـبـاحیں ہو

ایتھـے اوتھـے دوہیں جہـانیں سبھ فقر دیاں جائیں ہو

عـرش کـولـوں سے مـنزل اگّے باہو پـیا کم تنهـائیں ہو

Lovers purify themselves but once until Resurrection Day.

They remain in prayer, kneeling and bowing night and day.

Here and Hereafter—both worlds are places of poverty.

Many stages lie beyond the divine throne, Bahu, and lovers must

deal with them.

purify: Bahu is referring to the ablutions performed before each of the five daily prayers. Muslims are required to renew their state of ritual purity if they touch anything that is ritually impure or perform any bodily function. To say of someone that they need to purify themselves just once is to imply that they never stop praying.

divine throne: the divine throne is mentioned in the Qur'an, although there is no one explanation of what it means (since God has no physical body). It is often considered to be the final point of mystical attainment.

عــشــق دی بــازی هــر جــا کهیــڈی شــاه گدا ســلطانــاں هو
عــالم فــاضــل عــاقــل دانــا کردا چــا حــیــرانــاں هو
تنْبو کهوڑ لتهّا وچ دل دے چا جوڑیس خلوت خاناں هو
عشق امیر فقیر منینْدے باہو کیا جانے لوك بیگاناں هو

They played the game of love everywhere, kings, beggars,
and sultans.
It even amazes sages, scholars, and savants.
It pitched a tent and occupied my heart, making it a
meditation cell.
Rich and poor both believe in love, Bahu, what do the
heedless know?

عشق اسانوں لسیاں جاتا لتھّا مل مہاڑی ہو

ناں سووے ناں سون دیوے جیویں بال رہاڑی ہو

پوہ مانگھیں منگے خربوزے میں کتھّوں لیساں واڑی ہو

عقل فکر دیاں بھل گیاں گلاں باہو جد عشق وجائی تاڑی ہو

Love saw me weak and it came, taking over my home.

Like a fussy child, it will not sleep nor let me sleep.

It asks for watermelons in winter, where can I find them?

But all rational thoughts were forgotten, Bahu, when love

   clapped its hands.

عشق جنہاندے ہڈیں رچیا اوہ رہندے چپ چپاتی ہو
لوں لوں دے وچ لکھ زباناں اوہ پھردے گنگے باتے ہو
اوہ کردے وضو اسم اعظم دا تے دریا وحدت وچ نہاتے ہو
تدوں قبول نمازاں باہو جد یاراں یار پچھاتے ہو

They, in whose bones love finds a home, remain completely silent.

A hundred thousand tongues in every hair, but they wander

like mutes.

They perform purifications of the Greatest Name, and bathe in the

sea of unity.

Prayers are only answered, Bahu, when friends recognize a Friend.

عاشق سوئی حقیقی جہڑا قتل معشوق دے منے ہو
عشق ناں چھوڑے مُکھ ناں موڑے توڑے سے تلواراں کھنے ہو
جتوَل ویکھے راز ماہی دے لگے اوسے بنے ہو
سچّا عشق حسین علی دا باہو سر دیوے راز ناں بھنے ہو

A true lover is one who accepts death for the Beloved.

He doesn't desert love, nor turns his face, even if wounded by
many swords.

He halts and stands wherever he sees the Beloved's mysteries.

Bahu, true love is that of Husayn and 'Ali: to give away one's head
but never give away the secret.

Husayn and 'Ali: 'Ali (the cousin and son-in-law of the Prophet) and Husayn
('Ali's son) both met their deaths as martyrs. In addition to being highly revered
by Sufis, they are central figures in Shi'a Islam.

عشق سمندر چڑھ گیا فلك تے کِتوَل جہاز کچیوے ہو
عقل فکر دی ڈونڈی نوں چا پہلے پور بوڑیوے ہو
کڑکن کپڑ پوون لہراں جد وحدت وچ وڑیوے ہو
جس مرنے تھیں خلقت ڈردی باہو عاشق مرے تاں جیوے ہو

The sea of love has risen to the heavens, where will the ship

   drop anchor?

The boat of intellect and rationality should be sunk on its very

   first trip.

Whirlpools and tidal waves assail him when he enters the state

   of unity.

That death which people fear, Bahu, the lover dies it so that he

   might live.

drowning?
unrelated to
rest of poem

عشق دی بھاہ ہڈاں دا بالن عاشق بَیہ سکیندے ہو

گھت کے جان جگر وچ آرا ویکھ کباب تلیندے ہو

سرگردان پھرن ہر ویلے خون جگر دا پیندے ہو

ہوئے ہزاراں عاشق باہو پر عشق نصیب کھیندے ہو

The fire of love, fueled by bones: lovers sit and stoke it.

Look! Taking a knife to their hearts and souls they cook kebabs!

They wander in amazement all the time and drink blood from

    their spleens.

Thousands have been lovers, Bahu, but love is in the fortunes of

    only a few.

- very morbid

- eating from bodies

- destroy physical body

عشق دیاں اولڑیاں گلاں جہڑا شرع تھیں دور ہٹاوے ہو
قاضی چھوڑ قضائیں جاون جد عشق طمانچا لاوے ہو
لوک ایانے متیں دیون عاشقاں مت ناں بھاوے ہو
مُڑن محال تنہاں نوں باہو جنہاں صاحب آپ بلاوے ہو

Scholarly path?

The ways of love are backward, turning you far from the path.

Judges abandon judging when love gives them a slap.

Meddlesome people give advice; the advice doesn't please

the lovers.

Turning back is absurd, Bahu, for those whom the Master has

called to Himself.

p 103

عـاشق شـوہدے دل کھـڑایا آپ بھـی نـالے کھـڑیا ہو
کھـڑیا کھـڑیا ولیـا نـاہیں سنگ مـحبوباں دے رلیـا ہو
عقل فکر دیاں سب بھُل گئیاں جد عشقے نال جا ملیا ہو
میں قربان تنہاں توں باہو جنہاں عشق جوانی چڑھیا ہو

The wretched lover lost his heart and with it also lost himself.

Once lost, he was never found, and mixed in with his friends.

Everything intellectual and rational was forgotten when he went

    and encountered love.

My life goes to those, Bahu, who are possessed by love in

    their youth.

عـــشـق اســانـوں لِسـیـاں جـــاتـا کـرکــے آوے دہـــائی ہو
جِتوَل ویکھاں مینوں عشق دسیوے خالی جگہ ناں کائی ہو
مـرشد کـامل ایـــسا مـلیا جـــس دل دی تـاکی لاہی ہو
مـیـں قربـان اس مـرشد بـاہو جس دسیا بھـیت الـهی ہو

Love saw me weak and it launched a raid.

Everywhere I look I see love, there is no empty space.

I found a guide so perfect, he opened the window of my heart.

I give my life for that guide, Bahu, who told me the

    divine mystery.

love as an attacker

کلمیں دی کل تداں پیوسے جداں کلمیں دل نوں پھڑیا ہو
بے درداں نوں خبر ناں کائی دردمنداں گل مڑھیا ہو
کفر اسلام دی کل تداں پیوسے جداں بھن جگر وچ وڑیا ہو
میں قربان تنہاں توں باہو جنہاں کلماں صحی کر پڑھیا ہو

I grasped the meaning of the creed when the creed grabbed

my heart.

The ones without pain have no knowledge of it, but the

painstricken have wrapped it around their necks.

One understands the meaning of Islam and disbelief when the

creed rushes and enters the heart.

I give my life for those, Bahu, who have said the creed perfectly.

*the spirtual guide's role
-laundry man*

کامل مرشد ایسا ہووے جہڑا دھوبی وانگوں چھٹّے ہو

نال نگاہ دے پاک کریندا وچ سجّی صابن نال گھتّے ہو

میلیاں نوں کردیندا چِٹّا وچ ذرّہ میل ناں رکھّے ہو

ایسا مرشد ہووے باہو جہڑا لوں لوں دے وچ وسّے ہو

The perfect guide thrashes one like a laundryman beats clothes.

He purifies with his gaze, and he soaks one in bleach and soap.

He makes the dirty white and does not leave a speck of dirt.

One should have such a guide, Bahu, living in every cell of

   one's being.

کوک دلاّ متاں رب سنے چا دردمنداں دیاں آہیں ہو

سینہ میرا دردیں بھریا اندر بھڑکن بھاہیں ہو

تیلاں باجھ ناں بلن مشالاں درداں باجھ ناں آہیں ہو

آتش نال یاراناں لا کے باہو پھر اوہ سڑن کہ ناہیں ہو

Heart, cry out! Maybe the Lord will hear the sighs of the
   painstricken.

My breast is filled with pain, flames flicker within it.

Lamps do not light without wicks, nor sighs without pain.

Striking up a friendship with fire, Bahu, should they burn or not?

کلمے نال میں نہاتی دھوتی کلمے نال ویاہی ہو
کلمے میرا پڑھیا جنازہ کلمے گور سہائی ہو
کلمے نال بہشتیں جاناں کلمہ کرے صفائی ہو
مُڑن مُحال تنہاں نوں باہو جنہاں صاحب آپ بلائی ہو

With the creed I bathed and washed, with the creed I was
   betrothed.
The creed said my funeral, the creed decorated my grave.
With the creed I am going to paradise, the creed will cleanse me.
Turning back is impossible, Bahu, for those whom the Master has
   called to Himself.

گند ظلمات اندھیر غباراں راہ نیں خوف خطر دے ہو

مُکھہ آب حیات منوّر چشمے اوتے سائے زلف عنبر دے ہو

مُکھہ محبوب دا خانہ کعبہ جتھے عاشق سجدہ کردے ہو

دو زلفاں وچ نین مصلے جتھے چاروں مذہب ملدے ہو

مثل سکندر ڈھونڈن عاشق ہک پلک آرام ناں کردے ہو

خضر نصیب جنھاندے باہو اوہ گھُٹ اوتھے جا بھردے ہو

Dirt, darkness, and dust—the paths are filled with dread

and danger.

The Face is a luminescent fountain of life, shaded by black

ambergris.

The Beloved's face is the House of Ka'ba, where lovers

bow down.

Between the locks, the eyes are mosques where the four

schools meet.

The lovers search like Alexander, not resting for an instant.

Khizr is in the fortunes of those, Bahu, who gulp their fill

over there.

the four schools: this refers to the four legal schools (*mazhab*) of Sunni Islam.

Khizr: the mystical guide of the unseen realm, identified both with the prophet Elijah and with the one who accompanied Alexander in his quest for the fountain of life (alluded to in the second line).

گودڑیاں وچ جال جنہاں دی اوہ راتیں جاگن ادھیاں ہو

سك ماہی دی ٹكن ناں دینْدی لوك انھّے دینْدے بدیاں ہو

انـدر میرا حـق تپـایا اسـاں كھلیـاں راتیں كـڈھیاں ہو

تـن تھیں ماس جدا ہویا بـاہـو سـوكھ جھـلارے ہـڈیاں ہو

Those who live in patched robes stay awake half the night.

Longing for the Beloved allows them no rest; the unseeing cast

aspersions.

Truth set me on fire inside; I've passed many nights standing.

The flesh withered off my body, Bahu, it is my bare skeleton that

is swaying.

patched robes: a symbol of poverty, but also a specifically Sufi form of dress. A many-patched robe (khirqa-yi hazār mīkhī; literally, "robe of a thousand stripes") was given by masters to their disciples as a badge of advancement on the Sufi path.

truth: the term haqq refers to truth and reality in an absolute sense. It is also frequently a reference to God.

"لا يحتاج" جنهاں نوں ہویا فقر تنهاں نوں سارا ہو

نظر جنهاں دی کیمیا ہووے اوہ کیوں مارن پارا ہو

دوست جنهانْڈا حاضر ہووے دشمن لین ناں وارا ہو

نام فقیر تنهانْڈا باہو جنهاں ملیا نبی سوہارا ہو

Whoever experiences "I shall not want" has complete poverty.

Those whose sight is alchemy, why should they use quicksilver?

Those whose Friend is present, why should their enemy launch

an attack?

True mystics are those, Bahu, who have received a vision of

the Prophet.

I shall not want: Bahu writes the phrase in Arabic. It refers to the Sufi concept of *tawakkul,* or complete reliance on God.

quicksilver: Mercury was used in the alchemical process of trying to turn base metals into gold. The Sufi process of turning an ordinary human being into an accomplished mystic is sometimes referred to as alchemy in Sufi literature.

لِکھّن سکھیوئی تے لِکھ ناں جاتا کیوں کاغذ کیتو ضائعا ہو
قط قلم نوں مار ناں جانیں تے کاتب نام دھرایا ہو
سبھ صلاح تیری ہوسی کھوئی جاں کاتب دے ہتھ آیا ہو
صحیح صلاح تنہاں دی باہو جنہاں الف تے میم پکایا ہو

You learned writing but you never understood the meaning of

writing, so why did you waste the paper?

You never learned how to cut a reed pen, but you call

yourself a scribe.

All your penmanship will be judged wrong when it comes into the

Scribe's hands.

Only they have proper penmanship, Bahu, who perfect the *alif*

and the *mīm*.

never look
beyond the literal

alif and the *mīm:* see p. 4.

لوک قبر دا کرسن چارا لحد بناون ڈیرا ہو

چٹکی بھر مٹی دی پاسن کرسن ڈھیر اچیرا ہو

دے درود گھراں نوں ونجن کوکن شیرا شیرا ہو

بے پرواہ درگاہ رب باہو نہیں فضلاں باجھ نبیڑا ہو

People will select a grave-site and make a home for you in
the grave.

They will first place a pinch of earth, then raise the mound
up high;

Offering their prayers, return to their homes, and lament
"My lion! My lion!"

The Lord's home knows no care, Bahu, and you cannot live there
without an act of grace.

✱ bird imagery

مرشد میرا شہباز الہی ونج رلیا سنگ حبیباں ہو
تقدیر الہی چھکیاں ڈوراں کداں ملسی نال نصیباں ہو
کوہڑیاں دے دکھ دور کریندا کرے شفا مریضاں ہو
ہر اک مرض دا دارو تو ہیں باہو کیوں گھت نائیں وس طبیباں ہو

My guide is the divine falcon who has gone and joined up with

    his friends.

The divine will is pulling my strings, when will I have the fortune

    to meet him again?

He banishes the pain of lepers; he heals the sick.

You are the cure of each and every ailment, Bahu, so why do you

    place me in the hands of physicians?

✱ why doesn't God heal directly?

مرشد مکّه تے طالب حاجی کعبه عشق بنایا ہو

وچ حضور سدا ہر ویلے کریئے حجّ سوایا ہو

ہک دم میتھوں جُدا ناں ہووے دل ملنے تے آیا ہو

مرشد عین حیاتی باہو میرے لوں لوں وچ سمایا ہو

The guide is Mecca, the seeker the pilgrim, and love has made
  the Ka'ba.

Let us do the Hajj all the time, forever in the divine presence.

He is not separated from me for one breath, yet my heart is eager
  to meet him.

The guide is the fountain of life, Bahu, arrayed in my every cell.

میں کوجھی میرا دلبر سوہنا میں کیونکر اس نوں بھانواں ہو
ویہڑے ساڈے وڑدا ناہیں پئی لکھ وسیلے پانواں ہو
ناں میں سوہنی ناں دولت پلّے کیونکر یار مناواں ہو
ایہہ دکھ ہمیشاں رہسی باہو روندی ہی مر جانواں ہو

I am ugly and my Beloved beautiful—how can I be agreeable

    to Him?

He never enters my home though I use a hundred thousand ruses.

Neither am I beautiful nor have I wealth to display—how can I

    please my Friend?

This pain shall remain forever, Bahu, I will die crying.

beauty, ruses, wealth
don't please God

Bahu refers to himself in the feminine throughout this poem. See pp. 7–8 for a
discussion of the female representation of the Sufi lover.

نال کُسنگی سنگ ناں کریئے کُل نوں لاج ناں لائیے ہو

تُمّے تربوز مول ناں ہونڈے توڑے توڑ مکّے لے جائیے ہو

کانواں دے بچّے ہنس ناں تھینڈے توڑے موتی چوگ چگایئے ہو

کوڑے کھوہ ناں مِٹّھے ہونڈے باہو توڑے سے من کھنڈ دا پایئے ہو

May we never keep company with an unfaithful friend; may we
   never disgrace all.

Bitter melons never become watermelons, even if we take them all
   the way to Mecca.

Baby crows never become swans, no matter how many pearls we
   feed them.

Brackish wells never become sweet, Bahu, no matter how many
   sackfuls of sugar we add.

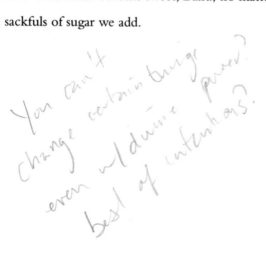

نہیں فقیری جلیاں مارن سُتیاں لوک جگاون ہو
نہیں فقیری وہندیاں ندیاں سُکیاں پار لنگھاون ہو
نہیں فقیری وچ ہوا دے مصلّیٰ پا ٹھہراون ہو
فقیری نام تنہانڈا باہو جھڑے دل وچ دوست ٹکاون ہو

Being a *faqir* is not dancing and whirling, waking up sleeping
  people.
Being a *faqir* is not crossing flowing streams without getting wet.
Being a *faqir* is not suspending a prayer mat in the air.
They are the real *faqirs,* Bahu, who nurture the Friend in
  their hearts.

— not miracle
  workers

نـاں رب عـرش مـعـلٰی اُتّے نـاں رب خـانے کـعـبے ہو
نـاں رب عـلم کـتـابیـں لـبّـا نـاں رب وچ مـحرابے ہو
گنگا تیر تھیں مول نـاں ملیا مارے پینڈے بے حسابے ہو
جـد دا مـرشـد پھـڑیـا بـاہـو چھُـتّـے سـب عـذابے ہـو

The Lord was neither found on the exalted throne, nor is the Lord
   in the Ka'ba.

The Lord was not found in learning and books, nor is the Lord in
   the prayer niche.

He was never found swimming in the Ganges, nor met through
   countless pilgrimages.

Ever since I held on to the guide, Bahu, I have been freed of all
   torments.

unrelated

---

prayer niche: the *mihrāb* is the niche in the front wall of a mosque which marks
the direction for prayer. It is often one of the architectural and decorative focal
points of a mosque.

ناں میں سُنّی ناں میں شیعہ میرا دوہاں توں دل سڑیا ہو

مُک گئے سبھ خشکی پینڈے جدوں دریا رحمت وچ وڑیا ہو

کئی من تارے ترتر ہارے کوئی کنارے چڑھیا ہو

صحیح سلامت چڑھ پار گئے باہو جنہاں مرشد دا لڑ پھڑیا ہو

Neither am I Sunni nor am I Shiʿa—my heart is bitter with both

    of them.

All long, dry marches came to an end when I entered the sea

    of mercy.

Many nonswimmers tried and lost; a few climbed the other bank.

They made it across safe and sound, Bahu, who clung to the

    guide's hem.

—not a faction

نـاں اوہ ہندو ناں اوہ مـومـن ناں سـجدہ دیـن مسیتی ہو
دم دم دے وچ ویکھـن مـولا جنہاں قـضا نـاں کیتی ہو
آہے دانے تے بنے دیوانے جنہاں ذات صحی ونج کیتی ہو
میں قربان تنہاں توں باہو جنہاں عشق بازی چُن لیتی ہو

They are neither Hindus nor Muslims, nor do they bow down in

the mosque.

With every breath they see the Lord, those who have never missed

a prayer.

They came sages and became madmen, those who truly understood

God's essence.

My life goes to those, Bahu, who have chosen the gamble of love.

[handwritten: # beyond religious titles?]

ناں میں جوگی ناں میں جنگم ناں میں چِله کمایا ہو

ناں میں بھج مسیتیں وڑیا ناں تسباح کھڑکایا ہو

"جو دم غافل سو دم کافر" مرشد ایہ فرمایا ہو

مرشد سوہنی کیتی باہو پل وچ جا پہنچایا ہو

Neither am I a yogi nor am I a dervish bard, nor have I completed

a forty-day retreat.

Neither have I rushed to enter a mosque nor have I rattled a

big rosary.

"Whoever is heedless for an instant is a disbeliever in an instant,"

so said my guide.

The guide has done a beautiful thing, Bahu, in an instant

transporting me there.

forty-day retreat: retreats and the use of rosaries are common Sufi practices.
A yogi is a Hindu mystic and a dervish a Muslim one.

ناں کوئی طالب ناں کوئی مرشد سب دلاسے مُٹھّے ہو

راہ فقر دا پرے پریرے سب حرص دنیا دے کٹھّے ہو

شوق الہی غالب ہویاں جند مرنے تے اُٹھّے ہو

باہو جیس تن بھڑکے بھا بربونڈی اوہ مرن تربارے بھکھّے ہو

They are neither seekers nor guides; they will all cause harm.

All those hungry for the world are to one side, the path of poverty

to the other.

The desire for the divine dominates them when they sit up just

before dying.

Those whose bodies dance with the fire of earthly desire, Bahu, die

thirsty and hungry.

نـیـڑے وسّـن دور دسـیـون ویـڑھے نـاہیـں وڑدے ہو
اندروں ڈھونڈن دا ول ناں آیا مورکھ باہروں ڈھونڈن چڑھدے ہو
دور گیـاں کـچھ حاصل نـاہیں شـوہ لـبھّے وچ گھـر دے ہو
دل کر صیقل شیشے وانگوں باہو دور تھـیـون کُل پردے ہو

They live near but appear far, never entering my courtyard.

They did not know how to search within, so the wretches began to
search without.

Nothing is gained by traveling afar, the Beloved is to be found in
one's home.

Burnish your heart like a mirror, Bahu, and all curtains will be
removed.

curtains: attaining mystical knowledge is often described as the removal of a
curtain or veil. Similarly, the metaphor of polishing the mirror of one's heart so
that it faithfully reflects the divine essence is commonly used in Sufism.

وحدت دے دریا اُچھلّے ہك دل صحی ناں کیتی ہو

ہك بُت خانے واصل تھیئے ہك پڑھ رہے مسیتی ہو

فاضل چھڈ فضیلت بیٹھے عشق بازی جاں لیتی ہو

ہرگز رب ناں ملدا باہو جنہاں ترٹی چوڑ ناں کیتی ہو

The seas of unity rose high, but not a heart was set right.

One attained union in the idol temple, while another remained
reading in the mosque.

Scholars abandoned scholarship when they gambled the game
of love.

The Lord is never found, Bahu, by those who do not risk
everything.

"ہو" دا جامہ پہن کراہاں اسم کماون ذاتی ہو
کفر اسلام مقام ناں منزل ناں اوتھے موت حیاتی ہو
شاہ رگ تھیں نزدیك لدھوسے پا اندرونی جھاتی ہو
اوہ اساں وچ اسیں انہاں وچ باہو دور رہی قرباتی ہو

Wearing the dress of "Hu," they earn the name "Of the Essence."

Islam and disbelief are neither stages nor goals, nor is there physical

    death over there.

I found Him closer than my jugular vein when I looked inside

    myself.

He is within me and I within Him, Bahu, intimacy remains distant.

Hu: lit. "He," referring to God. It is a very common formula repeated during the Sufi meditational exercise known as *zikr.* See pp. 4–5 for use of "hu" in Sultan Bahu's name.

closer than my jugular vein: one of the commonest ways of describing the immanence of God in Islam.

ہك جاگن ہك جاگ ناں جانن ہك جاگدیاں ہی سُتّے ہو

ہك ستیاں جا واصل ہوئے ہك جاگدیاں ہی مُٹھے ہو

کے ہویا جے گھگّو جاگے جہڑا لینْڈا ساہ اُپْٹھے ہو

میں قربان تنہاں توں باہو جنہاں کھوہ پریم دے جُتّے ہو

There are those who are awake, those who don't know how to be
   awake, and those who are asleep while waking.
There are those who attained union while sleeping, and those who
   were deprived of it while waking.
The stupid owl, who even breathes backward, so what if it
   stays awake?
My life goes to those, Bahu, who have worked the wells of love.

owl: a symbol of stupidity in South Asian culture.

ہک دم سجّن تے لکھ دم ویری ہک دم دے مارے مردے ہو

ہک دم پچھے جنم گوایا چور بنے گھر گھر دے ہو

لائیاں دا اوہ قدر کی جانن جہڑے محرم ناہیں سرّ دے ہو

سو کیوں دھکّے کھاون باہو جہڑے طالب سچّے در دے ہو

A friend for one breath and an enemy for a hundred thousand; for

    one breath's sake I am dying!

For one breath I lost a lifetime, became hated in every home.

What do those who don't share the secret know of the value

    of bonds?

And why should they suffer shoves, Bahu, those who seek the

    true doorway?

وحدت دا دریا الٰہی جتھّے عاشق لینْدے تاری ہو
مارن ٹُبیاں کڈھن موتی آپو آپسی واری ہو
دُرّ یتیم وچ لَئے لشکارے جیوں چَن لاٹاں ماری ہو
سو کیوں نہیں حاصل بھردے باہو جھڑے نوکر نیں سرکاری ہو

The sea of unity is divine where lovers take a swim.

They dive and bring out pearls, each in their own turn.

There are flashes in a rare pearl, like the moon giving off rays

   of light.

Then why do they not fulfill their duties, Bahu, those who are

   the King's servants?

کلمے لکھ کروڑاں تارے ولی کیتے سے راہیں ہو
کلمے نال بجھائے دوزخ جتھّے اگ بلے از گاہیں ہو
کلمے نال بہشتیں جاناں جتھّے نعمت سنج صباحیں ہو
کلمے جیہی ناں کوئی نعمت باہو اندر دوہیں سرائیں ہو

The creed has saved millions from drowning and turned travelers
   into saints.

The creed extinguishes hell, where an inescapable fire burns.

Through the creed, the heavens are alive with blessings night
   and day.

There is no blessing like the creed, Bahu, in both resting places.

both resting places: this world and the afterlife.

چڑھ چناں تے کر رشنائی ذکر کریندے تارے ہو
گلیاں دے وچ پھرن نماݨے لعلانڈے ونجارے ہو
شالا مسافر کوئی نہ تھیوے ککھ جنھاں توں بھارے ہو
تاڑی مار اڈاؤ ناں باہو اساں آپے اُڈن ہارے ہو

Arise and shine bright, moon! The stars are engaged in divine
   recollection.

Ruby merchants are wandering the alleys like wretches.

May no one ever be a traveler, whose weight is less than that
   of straw.

Don't clap your hands to make me fly, Bahu, I'm about to take
   flight on my own.

دل تے دفتـر وحـدت والا دائـم کـریں مطالعیـا ہو
ساری عمراں پڑھیـاں گزری جھَلاں دے وچ جالیـا ہو
ہکو اسـم اللّٰه دا رکّھیـں اپنا سبـق مطـالعیـا ہو
دوہیں جہان غلام تنہانڈے باہو جیں دل اللہ سنبھالیا ہو

The heart is a register of unity, so study it always.

Your entire life was spent in study, passed in ignorance.

Keep only the name "Allah" as your one lesson to contemplate.

Both worlds are slaves of those, Bahu, who guard Allah in

    their hearts.

گیا ایمان عشقے دیوں پاروں ہو کر کافر رہیے ہو

گھت زنّار کفر دا گل وچ بت خانے وچ بہیے ہو

جس خانے وچ جانی نظر ناں آوے اوتھے سجدہ مول ناں دیہے ہو

جاں جاں جانی نظر ناں آوے باہو توڑے کلماں مول ناں کہیے ہو

Faith left for the sake of love: let's live as disbelievers.

Hanging a thread of disbelief from our necks, let's sit in an

idol temple.

Where the Beloved cannot be seen, let's never bow down there.

Wherever the Beloved cannot be seen, Bahu, let's never recite the

creed there.

thread of disbelief: in Punjabi, *zunnār,* the sacred thread worn by Brahmin Hindus, serves as a symbol of non-Islamic religiosity among Indian Muslims. It also has similar connotations in other parts of the Islamic world, because it originally referred to the cloth belt worn by Persian Magis. This symbolic item of clothing was later imposed upon Eastern Christians and Jews to distinguish them from Muslims.

جل جلیندیاں جنگل بھونڈیاں میری ہکّا گل ناں پگّی ہو

چلے چلئے مکّے حجّ گزاریاں میری دل دی دوڑ ناں ڈکّی ہو

تریہے روزے پنج نمازاں ایہ بھی پڑھ پڑھ تھکّی ہو

سبھے مراداں حاصل ہویاں باہو جاں کامل نظر مہر دی تکّی ہو

Living in swamps and wandering in jungles, not one of my needs
was met.

I went to Mecca to make the Pilgrimage, but the racing of my
heart did not stop.

The thirty fasts and five daily prayers: these too I did until I
was tired.

All my wishes were fulfilled, Bahu, with one merciful glance of the
Perfect One.

thirty fasts: see p. 29.

تارک دنیا تد تھیوسے جداں فقر ملیوسے خاصا ہو

راہ فقر دا تد لدھیوسے جداں ہتھ پکڑیوسے کاسا ہو

دریا وحدت دا نوش کیتوسے اجاں بھی جی پیاسا ہو

راہ فقر رت ہنجوں روون باہو لوکاں بھانے ہاسا ہو

I abandoned this world when I found true needlessness.

I found the path of poverty when I held a begging bowl

    in my hand.

I drank up the sea of unity but still I am thirsty.

I cried tears of blood on this path, Bahu, but for others it is

    all a joke.

جو دم غافل سو دم کافر" اساں مرشد ایہ پڑھایا ہو"

سنیا سخن گیاں کھُل اکھّیں اساں چت مولا ول لایا ہو

کیتی جان حوالے رب دے اساں ایسا عشق کمایا ہو

مرن توں اگّے مر گئے باہو تاں مطلب نوں پایا ہو

"Whoever is heedless for an instant is a disbeliever in an instant,"

    so said my guide.

My eyes opened on hearing these words, and I turned my attention

    to the Lord.

I put my life in His trust—such is the love I gained.

I died before dying, Bahu, only then did I find my purpose.

لوہا ہوویں پیا کُٹیویں تاں تلوار سدیویں ہو
کنگھی وانگوں پیا چریویں تاں زلف محبوب بھریویں ہو
مہندی وانگوں پیا گھُٹیویں تاں تلی محبوب زنگیویں ہو
وانگ کپاہ پیا پنجیویں تاں دستار سَدیویں ہو
عاشق صادق ہوویں باہو تاں رس پریم دا پیویں ہو

Be steel, be beaten, only then will you be called a sword.

Like a comb, be sliced, only then will you be filled with the
Beloved's locks.

Like henna, be ground up, only then will you decorate the
Beloved's hands.

Like cotton, be carded, only then will you be called a turban
of honor.

Be a true lover, Bahu, only then will you drink the nectar of love.

— body of the Beloved

میں شہباز کراں پروازاں وچ دریا کرم دے ہو

زبان تاں میری "کُن" برابر موڑاں کم قلم دے ہو

افلاطون ارسطو جیہیں میرے اگے کس کم دے ہو

حاتم جیہیں لکھ کروڑاں در باہو دے منگدے ہو

I am a falcon, I fly in the sea of divine nobility.

My tongue is the equal of the divine command "Be!" and I change

the works of the Pen.

What good are the likes of Plato and Aristotle before me?

A hundred million like Hatim come begging at Bahu's door.

the divine command "Be!": according to Islamic tradition, "Be!" (*kun*) is the divine command God issued when He wished to begin the process of creation. The Pen refers to the divine pen with which God wrote down the destiny of all that He had created.

Hatim: Hatim at-Ta'i is a legendary Arab figure famous for his generosity and acts of chivalry. He is also popularly believed to be an ancestor of the famous Sufi Ibn al-'Arabi.

یار یگانہ ملسی تینوں جے سر دی بازی لائیں ہو

عشق اللّٰه وچ ہو مستانہ "ہو ہو" سدا الائیں ہو

نال تصوّر اسم اللّٰه دے دم نوں قید لگائیں ہو

ذاتے نال جاں ذاتی رلیا تد "باہو" نام سدائیں ہو

You will find the singular Beloved if you gamble your head.

Be drunk in the love of Allah, always saying "Hu! Hu!"

While contemplating the name of Allah, control your breath.

When essence blends with Essence, only then will you be called

   "Bahu."

Bahu: "Bahu" literally means "with Him." See pp. 4–5.

God lives inside of you

ایہ تن رب سچّے دا حُجرا وچ پا فقیرا جھاتی ہو
ناں کر منّت خواج خضر دی تیرے اندر آب حیاتی ہو
شــوق دا دیوا بال ہنیرے متاں لبھی وست کھڑاتی ہو
مرن تھیں اگّے مر رہے باہو جنہاں حق دی رمز پچھاتی ہو

This body of yours is the True Lord's dwelling, so mystic,

    look inside!

Don't beg favors from Master Khizr, the water of life is within you.

Illuminate the darkness with the lamp of longing, then perhaps

    you'll find what you have lost.

They die before they die, Bahu, those who understand the

    riddle of Truth.

BIBLIOGRAPHY

Ali, M. Athar. *The Mughal Nobility under Aurangzeb*. Rev. ed. Delhi: Oxford University Press, 1997.

Asani, Ali S., and Kamal Abdel-Malek. *Celebrating Muhammad: Images of the Prophet in Popular Muslim Poetry*. Columbia: University of South Carolina Press, 1995.

Babri, Laiq. *Sukhan kē wāris*. Islamabad: Lok Virsa, 1984.

Brass, Paul R. *Language, Religion and Politics in North India*. Cambridge and New York: Cambridge University Press, 1974.

Hamadani, Sayyid Ahmad Saʿid. *Ahwāl-u maqāmāt-i Hazrat Sultān Bāhū*. Edited by Hafiz M. Afzal Faqir. Islamabad: Islamic Book Foundation, 1991.

Hamid, Sultan. *Manāqib-i Sultānī*. Urdu translation by Malik Chunan al-din. Lahore: For the booksellers, n.d.

Krishna, L. R., and A. R. Luther. *Sultan Bahu: Sufi Poet of the Punjab*. Lahore: Sh. Mubarak Ali, 1982.

Mahmud, Sayyid Fayyaz. *Folk Romances of Pakistan*. Lahore: Lok Virsa and Sang-e Meel Publications, 1995.

Malik, Iftikhar H. "Identity Formation and Muslim Party Politics in the Punjab, 1897–1936: A Retrospective Analysis." *Journal of Modern Asian Studies* 29:2 (1995), 293–323.

Mirza, Shafqat Tanveer. *Resistance Themes in Punjabi Literature*. Lahore: Sang-e Meel Publications, 1992.

Narang, C. L. *History of Punjabi Literature, 850–1850 A.D.* Delhi: National Book Shop, 1987.

Qurayshi, Masʿud, trans. *ʿAks-i Bāhū: Sultān al-ʿārifin Hazrat Sultān Bāhū kē kalām kā urdū tarjuma*. Islamabad: Lok Virsa, 1980.

Rizvi, Saiyid Athar Abbas. *A History of Sufism in India*. 2 vols. New Delhi: Munshiram Manoharlal, vol. 1, 1978, rpt. 1986; vol. 2, 1983.

Shackle, C. "Language and Cultural Identity in Pakistan Punjab," in *Contributions to South Asian Studies,* vol. 1. Edited by Gopal Krishna. Delhi: Oxford University Press, 1979, 137–60.

———. "Punjabi in Lahore." *Journal of Modern Asian Studies* 4:3 (1970), 239–67.

———. "Siraiki: A Language Movement in Pakistan." *Journal of Modern Asian Studies* 11:3 (1977), 379–403.

———. "Some Observations on the Evolution of Modern Standard Punjabi," in *Sikh History and Religion in the Twentieth Century.* Edited by Joseph T. O'Connell, Milton Israel, W. G. Oxtoby, W. H. McLeod, and J. S. Grewal. South Asian Studies Papers, no. 3. Toronto: University of Toronto, Centre for South Asian Studies, 1990, 101–9.

Singh, Chetan. "Centre and Periphery in the Mughal State: The Case of Seventeenth-Century Panjab." *Journal of Modern Asian Studies* 22:2 (1988), 299–318.

Sultan Bahu. *Abyāt-i Bāhū.* With Urdu translation and commentary by Sultan Altaf Ali. Lahore: Al-Faruq Book Foundation, n.d.

———. *Abyāt-i Bāhū: Sultān al-ʿārifīn hazrat Sultān Bāhū kā majmūʿa-yi kalām.* Edited by Maqbul Anwar Daudi. Lahore: Feroze Sons, 1990.

———. *Chambe dī būtī: Sultāna Bāhū dā kalāma.* Edited by S. Dewindara. New Delhi: Sahitya Akademi, 1991.

———. *Kalām-i Sultān Bāhū.* Edited by Sayyid Nazir Ahmed. Lahore: Packages Ltd., 1981.

———. *Kalīd at-tawhīd kalān.* Urdu translation. Silsila-yi tasawwuf, no. 194. Lahore: Allāh wālē kī qawmī dukkān, n.d.

———. *Mahik al-faqr kalān.* Translated into Urdu by Malik Fazl Din Mujaddidi Naqshbandi. Lahore: Allāh wālē kī qawmī dukkān, n.d.

———. *Naqsh-i Bāhū: Hazrat Sultān Bāhū kā fārsī kalām awr urdū tarjama.* Translated into Urdu by Masʿud Qurayshi. Islamabad: Lok Virsa, n.d.

———. *Nūr al-hudā-yi kalān.* Edited and translated into Urdu by Faqir Nur Muhammad Sarwari Qadiri. Lahore: n.p., 1976.

———. *Of the Spirit (Ruhi) and Of the Spirit-Small (Ruhi Khoord).* Translated by S. A. Saeed Hamadani. Jhang, Pakistan: Hadrat Ghulam Dastgir Academy, 1996.

———. *The "Abyāt" of Sultān Bāhoo.* Edited and rendered into English by Maqbool Elahi. Lahore: Sh. Muhammad Ashraf, 1967.

Tafhimi, Sajidullah. "Shaykh Sultan Bahu: His Life and Persian Works." *Journal of the Pakistan Historical Society* 28:2 (1980), 133–50.

INDEX OF FIRST LINES

Designer: Barbara Jellow
Compositor: G & S Typesetters, Inc.
Text: 10.5/13.5 Bembo
Display: Bembo
Printer and Binder: Edward Brothers

Printed in the United States
88013LV00011B/51/A

9 780520 212428